A Generous Community
Buys Best Sellers

RIVERSIDE PUBLIC LIBRARY · FOUNDATION

2003 Annual
Community
Challenge
Campaign

WILLIAMS-SONOMA

FRENCH

RECIPES
DIANE ROSSEN WORTHINGTON

GENERAL EDITOR
CHUCK WILLIAMS

PHOTOGRAPHS
MAREN CARUSO

SIMON & SCHUSTER • **SOURCE**

NEW YORK • LONDON • TORONTO • SYDNEY • SINGAPORE

CONTENTS

THE CLASSICS

HORS D'OEUVRES, SOUPS, AND SALADS

VEGETABLES AND SIDE DISHES

SEAFOOD AND POULTRY

BEEF, VEAL, PORK, AND LAMB

DESSERTS

INTRODUCTION

When I first visited France, nearly 50 years ago, the simple and delicious dishes I tasted there made an impression on me that I've never forgotten. In fact, the French culinary traditions of using the best equipment and ingredients available and of mastering a few fundamental cooking techniques are part of what inspired me to create the first Williams-Sonoma store. Since then, I'm happy to report that these basic lessons of French cooking have become part of America's culinary heritage, as well.

The selection of recipes in this book represents the range of French cuisine today, such as regional specialties, bistro favorites, and updated classics—all easy to make and a pleasure to share at the table. Once you have mastered some of the basic French cooking techniques, explained at the back of this book, you will be able to apply this knowledge every time you cook. It is my hope that the recipes in this book will instill in you a love of the simple good food that has been part of the French way of life for centuries.

Chuck Williams

THE CLASSICS

A crisp-skinned roast chicken, a bowlful of mussels, a pile of golden pommes frites *alongside a steak coated with cracked pepper—these dishes convey the warmth and welcome of a classic bistro. Here, you will also find recipes for other time-honored French favorites, including a seaside-perfect* salade niçoise, *rich onion soup with Gruyère-topped croutons, and a lofty cheese soufflé.*

TWO-ONION SOUP GRATINÉE

In a large, nonaluminum Dutch oven or saucepan over medium heat, heat the olive oil. Add the red and yellow onions and sauté until wilted, about 15 minutes. Add the sugar and continue cooking, stirring frequently, until the onions are richly colored and caramelized, 30–45 minutes longer. (If the onions start to brown too quickly toward the beginning of the caramelizing process, you may need to reduce the heat slightly.)

Preheat the oven to 350°F (180°C).

Add the stock, garlic, bay leaf, and wine to the pan. Cover partially and simmer until the flavors are well blended, about 30 minutes.

Meanwhile, toast the baguette slices: Arrange the slices in a single layer on a baking sheet and toast in the oven until golden, watching carefully to prevent burning, 5–7 minutes.

Add the thyme to the soup and season to taste with salt and pepper. Discard the bay leaf.

To serve, preheat the broiler (grill). Ladle the soup into individual ovenproof soup bowls. Place 2 or 3 baguette slices on top of each serving and sprinkle evenly with the cheese. Place the soup bowls on a baking sheet and slide under the broiler about 4 inches (10 cm) from the heat source. Broil until the cheese is bubbly and lightly browned, 3–4 minutes. Sprinkle a little parsley over each soup bowl and serve at once.

MAKES 4–6 SERVINGS

GRUYÈRE CHEESE

A firm, nutty cow's milk cheese, Gruyère is actually a Swiss cheese named for the alpine region in which it originated, although it is also produced in France. The French version of this cheese is called Gruyère de Comté, or simply Comté. It is aged longer than Swiss Gruyère, and, as a result, has a deeper flavor. Other similar cheeses include French Beaufort and Swiss Emmental. With their robust flavor and smooth melting qualities, the cheeses of the Gruyère family make a perfect topping for gratinéed dishes such as this classic onion soup.

3 tablespoons olive oil

4 large red onions, thinly sliced

4 medium yellow onions, thinly sliced

¼ teaspoon sugar

7 cups (56 fl oz/1.75 l) beef or chicken stock (pages 110–11) or prepared low-sodium broth

2 cloves garlic, minced

1 bay leaf

½ cup (4 fl oz/125 ml) dry white wine

12 slices baguette, each ¼ inch (6 mm) thick

¼ teaspoon dried thyme leaves

Salt and freshly ground pepper

¾ cup (3 oz/90 g) shredded Gruyère cheese

2 tablespoons finely chopped fresh flat-leaf (Italian) parsley

POULET RÔTI

FOR THE RUB:

1 tablespoon coarsely chopped fresh rosemary

3 cloves garlic, minced

¼ cup (2 fl oz/60 ml) fresh lemon juice

4 tablespoons (2 oz/60 g) unsalted butter, at room temperature

⅛ teaspoon cayenne pepper

Pinch of paprika

Salt and freshly ground black pepper

1 roasting chicken, 3½–4 lb (1.75–2 kg), giblets reserved for another use, rinsed and patted dry

Whole fresh rosemary sprigs and thyme sprigs for garnish (optional)

Preheat the oven to 425°F (220°C). To make the rub, in a small bowl, mix together the chopped rosemary, garlic, lemon juice, butter, cayenne, paprika, and salt and black pepper to taste until well incorporated. Taste and adjust the seasoning.

Coat the chicken all over with the rub. Place, breast side up, on an oiled rack in a large, heavy roasting pan. Pour 1 cup (8 fl oz/250 ml) water into the pan to prevent the bottom from burning as juices drip from the chicken. (You may need to add more water to the pan bottom if it becomes dry during roasting.) Roast the chicken, basting several times with the pan juices, until golden brown, 45–50 minutes. An instant-read thermometer inserted into the thickest part of a thigh (but not touching bone) should register 170°F (77°C), and the juices should run clear when the thigh is pierced with a knife.

Let rest for about 10 minutes before carving. If desired, serve the chicken on a bed of rosemary and thyme sprigs.

Variation Tip: If you like, you can alter the herb mixture in this recipe. Substitute 1½ tablespoons chopped fresh tarragon or 1½ table-spoons chopped fresh thyme for the rosemary. Reduce the garlic to 2 cloves and omit the cayenne pepper and paprika.

Serving Tip: This simple main-course chicken is also ideal for use in sandwiches or to add to salads and pastas. Prepare the chicken in advance so that it is cool enough to slice, dice, or shred.

MAKES 4 SERVINGS

ROASTING SAVVY

A few basic roasting tools and tips will help you master this bistro staple. Many cooks like to use an oiled roasting rack because it elevates the chicken, allowing more of its surface to brown. This is not absolutely necessary, however. Using a bulb baster or a large spoon, baste the chicken with the pan juices as it roasts to prevent it from drying out too quickly as it cooks and to add flavor and color. Above all, do not over-cook the chicken. Use an instant-read thermometer to check for doneness, and remove the chicken from the oven as soon as it has finished roasting for the best results.

STEAK AU POIVRE

Using a mortar and pestle, a spice grinder, or the coarsest setting on a pepper mill, crush the peppercorns until coarsely ground. Sprinkle the pepper evenly on both sides of the steaks and press it into the meat, using your hands or the flat side of a cleaver blade. Cover and let stand for 30 minutes.

Select one large frying pan or two smaller frying pans big enough to fit the steaks without crowding. Melt the butter with the olive oil over medium-high heat until bubbling, about 1 minute. Add the steaks and sear on one side until browned, about 4 minutes. Turn the steaks and sear on the other side until browned and an instant-read thermometer inserted into the thickest part registers 125°F (52°C) for rare or 135°F (57°C) for medium-rare, about 5 minutes longer. Transfer the steaks to a warmed platter and cover loosely with aluminum foil.

Add the shallots to the pan and sauté, adding more butter if needed to prevent sticking, until softened, 2–3 minutes. Remove from the heat. Add the Cognac, return to medium-low heat, and cook to warm the Cognac, about 30 seconds. Once again, remove the pan from the heat. Make sure the overhead fan is off and, averting your face, use a long kitchen match to ignite the Cognac. When the alcohol has burned off, the flames will die out. (Keep a pan lid ready in case the flames flare up.) When the flames disappear, add the wine, bring to a boil, and cook until lightly thickened, about 3 minutes. Add the stock, return to a boil, and cook until reduced by half and thickened to a saucelike consistency, about 5 minutes longer. Whisk in the cream and mustard and simmer for 1 minute longer. Season to taste with salt and pepper.

Transfer the steaks to warmed individual plates and spoon some of the sauce over each serving. Garnish with the parsley and serve.

MAKES 4 SERVINGS

½ cup (2½ oz/75 g) black peppercorns

4 New York strip steaks, each about 1 lb (500 g) and 1½ inches (4 cm) thick

4 tablespoons (2 oz/60 g) unsalted butter, plus extra as needed

2 tablespoons olive oil

4 shallots, minced

3 tablespoons Cognac (page 113) or other high-quality brandy

½ cup (4 fl oz/125 ml) full-bodied red wine

1 cup (8 fl oz/250 ml) beef stock (page 111), prepared low-sodium beef broth, or purchased veal stock

½ cup (4 fl oz/125 ml) heavy (double) cream

1 teaspoon Dijon mustard

Salt and freshly ground pepper

Fresh flat-leaf (Italian) parsley sprigs for garnish

POMMES FRITES

4 russet potatoes, about 2 lb (1 kg) total weight

Vegetable oil, such as canola, for deep-frying

Kosher or coarse salt for sprinkling

Peel the potatoes and cut lengthwise into slices about ⅜ inch (1 cm) thick. Then, cut the slices lengthwise into strips about ⅜ inch (1 cm) thick. Transfer the potato strips to a bowl of cold water and let stand to remove excess starch, about 15 minutes.

Pour vegetable oil to a depth of 2 inches (5 cm) into a deep fryer or a large, heavy pot with a deep-frying thermometer attached to the side. Heat the oil over high heat until it registers 330°F (165°C). If you do not have a deep-frying basket, have ready a pair of long tongs or a large skimmer.

While the oil heats, drain the potatoes and dry them with kitchen towels. (Wet potatoes may splatter and stick together.) If using a deep fryer, first dip the basket into the hot oil to prevent the potatoes from sticking to it. Then, working in batches, carefully place 3 large handfuls of the potatoes into the pot. The oil will expand and should cover them. Fry until the potatoes are lightly golden but have not started to brown, 4–5 minutes. If using a deep fryer, remove the basket and set over a bowl to drain for at least 10 minutes, then transfer the drained potatoes to paper towels. If using tongs or a skimmer, transfer the potatoes to a platter lined with several layers of paper towels to drain. Between batches, let the oil return to 330°F and remove any potato bits. The partially fried potatoes will keep at room temperature for up to 2 hours.

Just before serving, reheat the oil to 370°F (188°C). Fry the potatoes again, in batches, until golden brown and crisp, 3–5 minutes. Drain on fresh paper towels. Transfer to a serving bowl or napkin-lined basket, season to taste with salt, and serve.

Caution: When deep-frying, do not heat the oil above 375°F (190°C). If it reaches 400°F (200°C) or more, it may start to smoke, then burst into flame.

MAKES 4 SERVINGS

ABOUT POMMES FRITES

To make irresistible bistro-style *pommes frites,* or French fries, start with fresh oil and use a thermometer to maintain a constant high temperature during frying. Also, dry the potatoes well and be careful not to crowd the pan. The true French secret to perfect *pommes frites,* however, is to fry the potatoes twice. The first low-heat frying cooks the insides, while a second hotter immersion creates a golden, crunchy exterior. Once cooked, *pommes frites* should be served immediately. Never cover them; their own steam will quickly turn them limp.

SALADE NIÇOISE

NIÇOISE OLIVES

Originating in Nice, on the Mediterranean coast of Provence, this summertime recipe has become a popular French favorite around the world. It's worth seeking out authentic small, dark, oval Niçoise olives, which are cured in brine and then packed in olive oil. They have a delectable meatiness and subtly briny flavor that add a unique taste to the mélange of southern French ingredients in the salad. Although native to Provence, Niçoise olives are also grown in Italy and Morocco.

Cut the carrots and bell pepper into julienne (page 38). Thinly slice the red onion and cut into 1½-inch (4-cm) pieces. Place the tuna in a small bowl and use a fork to break it up into chunks. Set aside.

In a small bowl, whisk together the lemon juice, mustard, garlic, and chervil. Slowly drizzle in the olive oil, whisking constantly until blended and thickened. Add salt and pepper to taste. Set the dressing aside.

In a large pot of boiling water, cook the potatoes until tender but slightly resistant when pierced with a fork, 20–30 minutes. Drain and let cool. When cool enough to handle, peel and cut into julienne. Place in a large bowl.

Bring a large saucepan three-fourths full of water to a boil. Add the green beans and cook until bright green and tender but slightly crisp, 5–7 minutes. Drain the beans, then plunge them into a bowl of ice water to stop the cooking. When cool, drain well, pat dry, and place in the bowl with the potatoes.

Add the carrots, bell pepper, red onion, olives, capers, chopped basil, pepper to taste, and half of the tuna to the bowl and toss to combine. Pour in just enough dressing to moisten the salad. Toss carefully to combine, making sure not to mash the potatoes. Taste and adjust the seasoning. Mound the salad high in a large, shallow bowl. Arrange the remaining tuna on the top of the salad. Spoon a little dressing on the tuna.

Cut the eggs into quarters lengthwise, and cut each tomato into 6 wedges. Garnish the salad with the egg quarters, tomato wedges, and basil leaves and serve. Pass the remaining dressing at the table.

MAKES 6 SERVINGS

2 carrots, peeled

1 small red bell pepper (capsicum), seeded

1 small red onion

3 cans olive oil–packed tuna, drained

⅓ cup (3 fl oz/80 ml) fresh lemon juice

2 teaspoons Dijon mustard

2 cloves garlic, minced

2 tablespoons finely chopped fresh chervil

⅔ cup (5 fl oz/160 ml) extra-virgin olive oil

Salt and freshly ground pepper

3 red potatoes, about 1 lb (500 g) total weight

1 lb (500 g) green beans, trimmed and cut into 1½-inch (4-cm) pieces

½ cup (2½ oz/75 g) Niçoise olives, drained and stemmed

2 tablespoons capers, preferably salt-packed, rinsed and drained

2 tablespoons finely chopped fresh basil, plus whole leaves for garnish

3 hard-boiled eggs, peeled

2 small tomatoes

CHEESE SOUFFLÉ

1 cup (4 oz/125 g) plus
2 tablespoons shredded
Gruyère or Comté cheese

2½ tablespoons unsalted
butter

3 tablespoons all-purpose
(plain) flour

1 cup (8 fl oz/250 ml)
whole milk

4 large egg yolks

1 teaspoon Dijon mustard

Salt and freshly ground
white pepper

Pinch of freshly grated
nutmeg

5 large egg whites

Pinch of cream of tartar

1 tablespoon fine fresh
(page 77) or dried bread
crumbs

Preheat the oven to 375°F (190°C). Butter a 6-cup (48–fl oz/1.5 l) soufflé dish and then coat the bottom and sides evenly with 1 tablespoon of the cheese.

In a saucepan over medium heat, melt the butter. Add the flour and mix with a wooden spoon for 1 minute. Cook until the mixture is bubbling but still white, about 2 minutes longer. While whisking constantly, add the milk. Bring to a simmer and continue to whisk until the sauce is thick and smooth, about 2 minutes longer. Remove from the heat and let cool for 10 minutes.

Add the egg yolks to the cooled milk mixture and whisk until smooth. Add the mustard, ½ teaspoon salt, a pinch of white pepper, and the nutmeg and whisk to combine.

In a large, spotlessly clean bowl, using a large balloon whisk or an electric mixer on medium speed, whip the egg whites with a pinch of salt and the cream of tartar until stiff peaks form. The peaks should stand upright on the whisk or beaters when lifted. Do not overbeat, or the whites will become rough and lumpy.

Using a rubber spatula, gently fold half of the egg whites into the milk mixture to lighten it. Gently stir in 1 cup of the remaining grated cheese and then fold in the remaining egg whites just until no white streaks remain. Scoop into the prepared dish and sprinkle with the remaining 1 tablespoon cheese and the bread crumbs.

Bake until the soufflé is puffed and the top is browned, 30–35 minutes. Serve at once.

MAKES 4 SERVINGS

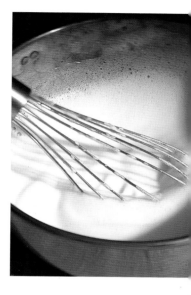

BEATING EGG WHITES

Soufflés have a reputation for being difficult to prepare, but by paying attention to a few details, you can create a successful soufflé every time. Start with a spotlessly clean bowl and large balloon whisk, as even a bit of grease can keep the whites from expanding properly. Adding a pinch of cream of tartar helps stabilize the foam, as does using an unlined copper beating bowl. When folding the whites into the soufflé base, use a rubber spatula in a gentle, sweeping under-and-over motion. Try to keep the egg whites as puffy as possible; the final mixture doesn't need to be uniform.

MOULES MARINIÈRE

In a large stockpot over medium-high heat, combine the wine, shallots, butter, 2 tablespoons of the parsley, the bay leaf, and pepper to taste. Bring to a simmer, add the bread crumbs, and cook, uncovered, until the broth is aromatic, 4–5 minutes.

Add the mussels, discarding any that do not close to the touch. Cover the pot tightly and steam the mussels, shaking the pot occasionally so they cook evenly, until they open, about 5 minutes. Discard any mussels that fail to open.

To serve, using a slotted spoon, transfer the mussels to large individual soup bowls. Ladle some of the broth over them and sprinkle with the remaining 2 tablespoons parsley. Serve at once, with bread for dipping into the broth.

Serving Tip: These classically prepared mussels are also delicious served with crisp Pommes Frites (page 17).

MAKES 6 FIRST-COURSE SERVINGS OR 2 MAIN-COURSE SERVINGS

Ingredients

2 cups (16 fl oz/500 ml) dry white wine

6 shallots, minced

6 tablespoons (3 oz/90 g) unsalted butter

4 tablespoons (⅓ oz/10 g) finely chopped fresh flat-leaf (Italian) parsley

½ bay leaf

Freshly ground pepper

1 cup (2 oz/60 g) fine fresh bread crumbs (page 77)

4 lb (2 kg) black or New Zealand green-lipped mussels, scrubbed and debearded *(far left)*

Crusty French bread for serving

MUSSELS

When choosing mussels, select those with tightly closed shells (open shells can mean the mussel inside is deteriorating or dead). To store, place the mussels in a deep bowl and cover with a damp kitchen towel; refrigerate for up to 1 day. Before cooking, scrub the shells with a stiff-bristled brush under cold running water. Using a small knife or scissors, cut off the beard, a fibrous tuft at the edge of the shell often present in locally harvested wild mussels. Cultivated mussels, the variety you find today in most fish markets, have little or no beards and are easier to clean.

HORS D'OEUVRES, SOUPS, AND SALADS

The charm of a French meal is evident from the very beginning. Who could resist a wedge of caramelized onion tart, or a sweet yet earthy salad of endives, beets, and goat cheese? Some of these dishes, such as the simple salad of frisée with bacon or the vegetable-laden pesto soup, could also serve as a light meal all on their own, paired with a fresh baguette and a glass of wine.

CARAMELIZED ONION TART

CARAMELIZED ONIONS

Onions contain natural sugars that remain hidden in their pungent, raw state. However, long, slow cooking brings these sugars out in a process called caramelization. For this recipe, thinly slice 6 large yellow onions. In a very large, deep frying pan over medium heat, melt 1 tablespoon unsalted butter with ¼ cup (2 fl oz/60 ml) olive oil. Add the onions, 1 teaspoon sugar, ½ teaspoon salt, and a sprinkle of freshly ground pepper. Cook, stirring often and reducing the heat if the onions brown too quickly, until the onions are richly colored, 40–45 minutes. Taste and adjust the seasoning.

To make the pastry, combine the flour and salt in a food processor. Pulse for a few seconds to blend. Add the butter and process until the mixture resembles coarse meal, 5–10 seconds. With the motor running, slowly add the ice water and process just until the dough comes together and adheres when pinched. Transfer the dough to a floured work surface and bring together into a rough mass. Press into a slightly flattened rectangular shape and roll out into a rectangle large enough to fit an 11-by-8-inch (28-by-20-cm) tart pan with a removable bottom. Alternatively, press the dough into a round disk and roll out into a circle large enough to fit an 11-inch (28-cm) round tart pan with a removable bottom. Drape the dough over the rolling pin and position it over the pan. Unroll the dough and ease it into the pan, pressing it against the sides and bottom without stretching. Trim off any excess dough by gently running the rolling pin across the top of the pan. Prick the dough with a fork and refrigerate until firm, about 30 minutes.

Preheat the oven to 375°F (190°C). Place the tart pan on a baking sheet. Line the dough with parchment (baking) paper and fill with pie weights, raw rice, or dried beans. Bake just until very light brown, 20–25 minutes. Let cool completely on a wire rack and remove the weights and paper. Brush the shell with the mustard and sprinkle with 2 tablespoons of the cheese. Return to the oven and bake until the cheese is melted, about 7 minutes. Let cool completely. Reduce the oven temperature to 350°F (180°C).

In a bowl, beat together the eggs, cream, thyme, and ½ cup (2 oz/ 60 g) of the cheese. Add the caramelized onions and stir to combine. Spoon into the tart shell and sprinkle with the remaining cheese. Bake until the cheese is melted and the filling is set, 30–35 minutes. Let cool. Remove the sides of the pan and transfer the tart to a serving plate. Serve warm or at room temperature.

MAKES 8 SERVINGS

FOR THE PASTRY:

1⅓ cups (7 oz/220 g) all-purpose (plain) flour

¼ teaspoon salt

½ cup (4 oz/125 g) very cold unsalted butter, cut into small pieces

¼ cup (2 fl oz/60 ml) ice water

2 tablespoons Dijon mustard

¾ cup (3 oz/90 g) shredded Gruyère cheese

2 large eggs

⅓ cup (3 fl oz/80 ml) heavy (double) cream

1½ teaspoons finely chopped fresh thyme or ½ teaspoon dried

Caramelized Onions *(far left)*, at room temperature

RILLETTES DE CANARD

1 Long Island, or White Pekin, duck, about 5 lb (2.5 kg), thawed if frozen, giblets discarded or reserved for another use

6 cloves garlic, chopped

1 bay leaf, crumbled

1 fresh thyme sprig, coarsely chopped, or ½ teaspoon dried thyme

Kosher salt and freshly ground pepper

Baguette or French bread slices or small crackers for serving

Pull the fat out of the duck cavity and set aside. Using a sharp knife, remove the breasts and reserve for another use. Remove the legs and thighs and set aside. Trim off the fat and any loose skin from the duck carcass and add to the reserved fat. Reserve the carcass.

Place the duck legs and thighs in a dish just large enough to hold them in a single layer. In a small bowl, toss together the garlic, bay leaf, thyme, 1 teaspoon salt, and ¼ teaspoon pepper. Rub the mixture over the legs and thighs. Cover and refrigerate overnight.

Chop the reserved fat coarsely and place in a large, heavy frying pan with the carcass. Add water to a depth of ½ inch (12 mm). Bring to a boil over medium heat. Reduce the heat to low and cook, stirring once or twice during the first 10 minutes, until the fat is melted and golden, about 45 minutes. Strain through a fine-mesh sieve lined with cheesecloth (muslin). Discard the solids. Let cool, then refrigerate the rendered fat.

Rinse the duck legs and thighs under cold running water, discarding the garlic and herbs. Reheat the rendered fat until melted. Place the legs and thighs in a small frying pan and add melted fat to cover. Bring to a simmer over medium heat. Reduce the heat to low, cover, and cook until the meat is tender and shreds easily, about 1 hour. Using a slotted spoon, transfer the duck pieces to a work surface. Strain the fat into a heatproof container and set aside until cool but still liquid. When the duck pieces are cool enough to handle, remove and discard the skin and bones and place the meat in a bowl. Using 2 forks, shred the meat. Mix in ½ cup (4 fl oz/125 ml) of the reserved fat. Season with salt and pepper and pack into a 1-cup (8–fl oz/250-ml) ramekin. Pour enough of the remaining fat over the top to seal. Refrigerate for at least 2 days to blend the flavors. Serve at room temperature, with the bread or crackers.

MAKES ABOUT 1 CUP (8 OZ/250 G)

DUCK FAT

Duck fat is a prized element in French cooking, but the roots of its use lie in simple farmhouse thriftiness. Duck has a thick layer of fat under its skin that must be rendered, or melted away, during cooking. The fat is delicious not only for frying eggs or potatoes, but also for cooking and preserving the duck itself. You can purchase rendered duck fat at specialty shops or gourmet butchers, or you can render it yourself (see recipe). Once the rillettes are prepared, they will keep in the refrigerator for up to 2 months.

POTAGE CRÉCY

In large soup pot over medium heat, melt the butter with the olive oil. Add the leeks and sauté, stirring occasionally, until softened, about 4 minutes. Add the carrots and potatoes and sauté just until they begin to soften, about 5 minutes.

Pour in the stock and bring to a simmer. Add the thyme, cover, and simmer until the carrots and potatoes are tender, about 25 minutes.

In a blender or food processor, purée the soup in batches and return the purée to the pot. Alternatively, process with a handheld blender in the pot. Add the half-and-half, lemon juice, nutmeg, and salt and white pepper to taste and bring to a simmer. Taste and adjust the seasoning.

Ladle the soup into warmed bowls and garnish with the thyme leaves, if using. Serve at once.

Note: French soups can be divided into four basic categories. A potage is a hearty, robust mixture, often puréed, while a soupe is usually made by simmering diced vegetables or other flavorings in stock. Smooth, velvety bisques, most often made with lobster or shellfish, are enriched with cream. Finally, a consommé is a clear broth that can be dressed up with any number of garnishes, from tiny dumplings to a sprinkling of chives.

MAKES 6 SERVINGS

POTAGE CRÉCY

Many French dishes are named in honor of their place of origin. Crécy, a town in northern France that produces some of the country's best carrots, is commemorated in every dish in which carrots are a star ingredient. When choosing carrots, look for firm, smooth ones without cracks or green spots. Smaller, slender but mature carrots, especially those that have been organically grown, have the best flavor. Very large or thick carrots often develop tough, woody cores, while immature baby carrots lack natural sweetness.

2 tablespoons unsalted butter

1 tablespoon olive oil

2 leeks, including tender green parts, rinsed (page 45) and thinly sliced

6–8 carrots, about 1½ lb (750 g) total weight, peeled and diced

2 large russet potatoes, about 1½ lb (750 g) total weight, peeled and diced

5 cups (40 fl oz/1.25 l) chicken stock (page 110) or prepared low-sodium broth

2½ teaspoons finely chopped fresh thyme or 1¼ teaspoons dried

2 cups (16 fl oz/500 ml) half-and-half (half cream)

2 tablespoons fresh lemon juice

½ teaspoon freshly grated nutmeg

Salt and freshly ground white pepper

1 tablespoon fresh thyme leaves or finely chopped fresh flat-leaf (Italian) parsley (optional)

SOUPE AU PISTOU

2 tablespoons olive oil

2 yellow onions, finely chopped

4 carrots, peeled and cut into 1-inch (2.5-cm) pieces

4 zucchini (courgettes), cut into 1-inch (2.5-cm) pieces

½ lb (250 g) young green beans, trimmed and cut into 1-inch (2.5-cm) pieces

¼ lb (125 g) white button mushrooms, brushed clean and thinly sliced

2 cloves garlic, minced

2 large tomatoes, peeled, seeded, and finely chopped, or 1 cup (6 oz/ 185 g) drained canned diced tomatoes

8 cups (64 fl oz/2 l) chicken stock (page 110) or prepared low-sodium broth

2 tablespoons finely chopped fresh basil or 1 tablespoon dried

1 can (15 oz/470 g) white beans such as cannellini, well rinsed and drained

Salt and freshly ground pepper

Pistou *(far right)* for serving

In a large soup pot over medium heat, heat the olive oil. Add the onions and sauté, stirring occasionally, until softened, 3–5 minutes.

Add the carrots, zucchini, and green beans and sauté, stirring frequently, just until softened, about 3 minutes. Add the mushrooms and sauté until coated with the oil, about 2 minutes. Add the garlic and sauté for 1 minute.

Raise the heat to medium-high, add the tomatoes, stock, and basil, and bring to a boil. Reduce the heat to medium and simmer until the vegetables are tender, about 15 minutes. The soup will be slightly thickened.

Add the white beans and cook until they are heated through, about 5 minutes. Add salt and pepper to taste.

Ladle the soup into warmed bowls and add a dollop of *pistou* to each bowl. Serve at once.

Make-Ahead Tips: This soup can be frozen for up to 2 months. To reheat, let the soup thaw at room temperature, then heat gently over medium heat. You can also omit the cheese from the pistou *and freeze the* pistou *for up to 2 months. Add the cheese just before serving.*

MAKES 8 SERVINGS

PISTOU

In the summertime in France, no vegetable soup is complete without a dollop of *pistou*. Unlike its Italian cousin, Genoese pesto, *pistou* contains no pine nuts, which makes it lighter. To make *pistou*, in a food processor, combine 2 cloves garlic, 2 cups (2 oz/60 g) packed fresh basil leaves, and ½ cup (½ oz/15 g) fresh flat-leaf (Italian) parsley leaves. Process until finely chopped. With the motor running, slowly pour in ½ cup (4 fl oz/125 ml) olive oil. Add ¼ teaspoon freshly ground pepper and ¾ cup (3 oz/90g) grated Parmesan cheese. Process until blended. Taste and adjust the seasoning. Makes about 1½ cups (12 fl oz/375 ml).

CHILLED ARTICHOKES WITH MUSTARD VINAIGRETTE

Working with 1 artichoke at a time and using a serrated knife, cut about ½ inch (12 mm) off the top of an artichoke to remove the main cluster of thorns. Pull the small leaves off the bottom near the stem and discard. Trim the stem flush with the bottom. Using scissors, trim ½ inch (12 mm) off the top of the outer leaves, removing the thorny tips. Drop into a large bowl of cold water to which you have added the lemon juice to prevent discoloration while you trim the remaining artichokes.

Fill a large saucepan or pot half full of water, add the white vinegar and olive oil, and bring to a boil over high heat. Add the artichokes, cover, and simmer until the bottoms are easily pierced with the tip of a knife, 40–50 minutes. (Smaller artichokes will cook a bit faster.)

Using tongs, transfer the artichokes, stem sides up, to a rack to drain as they cool. Invert onto a platter, cover, and refrigerate until chilled, at least 4 hours.

To make the vinaigrette, in a small bowl, whisk together the red wine vinegar, lemon juice, mustard, shallot, garlic, parsley, and chives. Slowly drizzle in the olive oil, whisking continuously until blended and thickened. Add salt and pepper to taste.

To serve, place the artichokes on a platter or individual plates and spoon some of the vinaigrette on top. Serve the remaining vinaigrette alongside. If desired, cut the large artichokes in half before serving.

Variation Tip: These artichokes are also delicious served warm with the vinaigrette.

MAKES 4 SERVINGS

ARTICHOKES

Different types of artichokes are cultivated in France, from the large-sized, purple-tinged Camus variety of Brittany to the smaller-headed artichokes of Provence. To eat a cooked whole artichoke, pull the leaves off one by one, dip the base of each leaf in the vinaigrette, and remove the flesh at the bottom of the leaf by scraping it between your teeth. Discard the leathery upper portion. Use a spoon to scrape out the hairy "choke" from the center, then cut the delicious heart into bite-sized pieces and dip in the vinaigrette.

4 large or 6 smaller artichokes

Juice of 1 lemon

2 tablespoons white vinegar

1 teaspoon olive oil

FOR THE VINAIGRETTE:

3 tablespoons red wine vinegar

1 tablespoon fresh lemon juice

2 teaspoons Dijon mustard, preferably whole grain

1 shallot, finely chopped

1 clove garlic, minced

1 tablespoon finely chopped fresh flat-leaf (Italian) parsley

1 tablespoon finely chopped fresh chives

¾ cup (6 fl oz/180 ml) extra-virgin olive oil

Salt and freshly ground pepper

SALADE FRISÉE AUX LARDONS

1 cup (2 oz/60 g) cubed coarse country bread (1-inch/2.5-cm cubes)

1½ tablespoons extra-virgin olive oil

Salt and freshly ground pepper

¾ lb (375 g) thick-cut bacon, cut into ½-inch (12-mm) pieces

2 shallots, finely chopped

5 tablespoons (2½ fl oz/ 75 ml) red wine vinegar

1 teaspoon white wine vinegar

4 large eggs

2 heads frisée, cored and leaves torn into 3-inch (7.5-inch) pieces

Preheat the oven to 350°F (180°C). Spread the bread cubes on a baking sheet and sprinkle them with the olive oil and salt and pepper. Place in the oven and toast, turning once or twice, until golden, about 15 minutes. Set aside.

In a frying pan over medium-high heat, sauté the bacon pieces, stirring occasionally, until crisp, 4–5 minutes. Add the shallots and sauté until softened, about 1 minute. Add the red wine vinegar, reduce the heat to medium, and simmer until slightly thickened, about 1 minute longer. Season to taste with salt and pepper. Set aside and keep warm.

Pour 6 cups (48 fl oz/1.5 l) water into a large, deep frying pan or wide saucepan and add 1 teaspoon salt and the white wine vinegar. Bring to a simmer over high heat. Reduce the heat to medium to maintain a gentle simmer. Break 1 egg into a ramekin and slide it carefully into the simmering water. Working quickly, repeat with the remaining 3 eggs. Carefully spoon the simmering water over the eggs until the whites are just opaque and firm and the yolks are still soft, about 3 minutes. Using a slotted spoon, transfer the eggs to a plate and set aside.

In a large salad bowl, combine the croutons and the frisée. Pour the warm dressing with the bacon pieces over the salad and toss to coat evenly. Divide the greens among shallow individual bowls, making sure there is an equal amount of bacon in each salad. Place a poached egg on top of each serving and serve at once.

Note: Poached eggs are not fully cooked. For more information, see page 113.

MAKES 4 SERVINGS

LARDONS

The French term *lardons* refers to small strips or squares of fat cut from the belly of a pig. They are often sautéed until crunchy and added to salads (such as this one) and other dishes, including stews, fried potatoes, and omelets. The same term is used for strips of pork fat that are inserted into leaner cuts of meat with a larding needle to increase tenderness and moisture. In the United States, slab bacon (rind removed), which comes from the side of the pig, is a good substitute for the pork fat. Salt pork, which comes from the belly of the pig, can also be used.

ENDIVE SALAD WITH ROASTED BEETS AND GOAT CHEESE

Preheat the oven to 425°F (220°C). If the beet greens are intact, cut them off, leaving about 1 inch (2.5 cm) of the stem. Place the unpeeled beets in a roasting pan and add water to a depth of ¼ inch (6 mm). Cover the pan tightly with aluminum foil.

Roast the beets until tender when pierced with a fork, about 45 minutes. Remove the beets from the pan and, when just cool enough to handle, use a small, sharp knife to remove the skins. Cut the beets into julienne *(left)*. Set aside.

In a small bowl, whisk together the vinegar, lemon juice, mustard, and shallot. Slowly drizzle in the olive oil, whisking continuously until blended and thickened. Add salt and pepper to taste.

In a large bowl, toss the endive with half of the dressing. Divide the endive among individual plates and scatter the beets and goat cheese on top. Sprinkle with pepper and garnish with the parsley. Pass the remaining dressing at the table.

MAKES 4–6 SERVINGS

JULIENNE

Julienne is the French term for foods, usually vegetables, cut into uniform, matchstick-shaped strips. To julienne the beets in this recipe, cut them into slices about ¼ inch (6 mm) thick. Stack the slices and, if desired, trim off the rounded edges to form an even square. Cut the beet slices lengthwise into strips about ¼ inch (6 mm) thick. You can also slice the beets on a mandoline (page 114).

2 beets

2 tablespoons balsamic vinegar

2 tablespoons fresh lemon juice

1 tablespoon Dijon mustard, preferably whole grain

1 shallot, finely chopped

½ cup (4 fl oz/125 ml) extra-virgin olive oil

Salt and freshly ground pepper

8 heads Belgian endive (chicory/witloof), cored and thinly sliced lengthwise

½ cup (2½ oz/75 g) crumbled fresh goat cheese

Finely chopped fresh flat-leaf (Italian) parsley for garnish

VEGETABLES AND SIDE DISHES

The open-air markets of France are a living connection to a country rich in agricultural history. Whether dining in or out, the French know that spring has arrived when the first slender shoots of asparagus appear, and that summer brings the delights of tender green beans. Even the cool days of autumn and winter can be sweetened with golden wedges of roasted fennel or a bubbling gratin of potatoes, cheese, and stock.

ROASTED ASPARAGUS WITH HAZELNUT OIL VINAIGRETTE

Preheat the oven to 350°F (180°C). Spread the hazelnuts in an even layer on a baking sheet and bake, stirring occasionally to color evenly, until the nuts are fragrant and the skins begin to split, about 10 minutes. Remove from the oven, wrap the still-warm nuts in a kitchen towel, and rub vigorously to remove the skins. Do not worry if bits of skin remain. Chop coarsely and set aside.

In a small bowl, whisk together the hazelnut oil, 3 tablespoons of the olive oil, the vinegar, ¼ teaspoon salt, and ⅛ teaspoon pepper until well blended. Set aside.

Raise the oven temperature to 450°F (230°C). If the skin on the asparagus seems thick and tough, peel the spears to within about 2 inches (5 cm) of the tips. Place the asparagus on a baking sheet and toss with the remaining 1 tablespoon olive oil and some salt and pepper, coating them evenly.

Roast the asparagus until the spears are tender and very lightly browned, about 12 minutes. Slender spears will cook more quickly; do not overcook.

Transfer the asparagus to a warmed platter and drizzle with the vinaigrette. Sprinkle with the toasted hazelnuts and serve warm.

MAKES 4 SERVINGS

½ cup (2½ oz/75 g) hazelnuts (filberts)

3 tablespoons hazelnut oil

4 tablespoons (2 fl oz/60 ml) extra-virgin olive oil

2 tablespoons white wine vinegar

Salt and freshly ground pepper

1½ lb (750 g) asparagus spears, tough ends removed

LEEKS VINAIGRETTE

8 leeks, about 3 lb (1.5 kg) total weight, including tender green parts, roots trimmed but intact

3 tablespoons olive oil

1½ cups (12 fl oz / 375 ml) chicken stock (page 110) or prepared low-sodium broth

2 tablespoons finely chopped fresh flat-leaf (Italian) parsley, plus extra for garnish

1 tablespoon fresh lemon juice

1½ teaspoons Dijon mustard

Salt and freshly ground pepper

Cut the leeks in half lengthwise, making sure the roots keep the leek halves together, and rinse thoroughly *(right)*.

In a frying pan large enough to fit the leeks in a single layer, heat 2 tablespoons of the olive oil over medium-high heat. Arrange the leeks in the pan and sauté, using tongs to turn them occasionally, until lightly browned, about 5 minutes. Add the stock and the 2 tablespoons parsley and bring to a simmer. Cover and cook until the leeks are tender when pierced with a sharp knife, about 10 minutes longer. Transfer the leeks to a serving platter.

Add the remaining 1 tablespoon olive oil, the lemon juice, and the mustard to the frying pan over medium heat and whisk to combine. Season to taste with salt and pepper. Pour the vinaigrette over the leeks and garnish with parsley. Serve at once.

Serving Tip: These leeks are also excellent served chilled. Cover and refrigerate for at least 4 hours or up to overnight.

MAKES 4–6 SERVINGS

LEEKS

Leeks are an integral part of the French *potager,* or "kitchen garden." Their mild onion flavor and silky texture make them a popular first course or side dish. Since leeks grow best in sandy soil, they need careful rinsing to get rid of the grit that lodges between the leaves. To rinse leeks, trim the root ends but leave them intact. Trim off the dark green leaf tops, then peel off any discolored outer leaves from the stalk. Split the leeks lengthwise and rinse carefully under cold water, gently spreading the layers apart to wash out any dirt.

HARICOTS VERTS
WITH SHALLOT AND LEMON

Bring a large saucepan three-fourths full of water to a boil. Add the beans and cook until bright green and tender but still slightly resistant to the bite, 5–7 minutes. Drain the beans, then plunge them into a bowl of ice water to stop the cooking. Drain well and set aside.

In a frying pan over medium heat, heat the olive oil. Add the shallot and sauté until softened, about 2 minutes. Raise the heat to medium-high, add the green beans, and sauté just until they begin to brown, about 2 minutes. Stir in the lemon zest and cook for 30–60 seconds longer. Remove from the heat and season to taste with salt and pepper. Transfer the beans to a warmed serving dish, garnish with the parsley, and serve at once.

MAKES 4–6 SERVINGS

1½ lb (750 g) haricots verts *(far left)*, stem ends trimmed

2 tablespoons olive oil

1 shallot, minced

1 teaspoon finely chopped lemon zest

Salt and freshly ground pepper

1 tablespoon finely chopped fresh flat-leaf (Italian) parsley

HARICOTS VERTS

French green beans, called *haricots verts,* are much slimmer and more delicate in flavor than most other varieties. Many specialty growers outside of France now cultivate these beans, so look for them at local farmers' markets in the summertime. Otherwise, use the slimmest, tenderest green beans you can find to make this side dish.

ROASTED FENNEL

4 fennel bulbs, about ¾ lb (375 g) each, trimmed and quartered, with some feathery fronds reserved for garnish

10 cloves garlic, peeled but left whole

3 tablespoons olive oil

Salt and freshly ground pepper

Preheat the oven to 425°F (220°C).

In a shallow roasting pan, combine the fennel, garlic cloves, and olive oil. Sprinkle with salt and pepper and toss until the fennel is evenly coated.

Roast, turning the fennel pieces and garlic cloves about every 20 minutes, until the fennel is softened, nicely browned, and caramelized, about 1 hour. Transfer to a warmed serving dish, garnish with the reserved fennel fronds, and serve at once.

Serving Tip: This dish is excellent served alongside Poulet Rôti (page 13), Sole Meunière (page 56), or Filets Mignons with Roquefort Sauce (page 81).

MAKES 4–6 SERVINGS

FENNEL

Along the Mediterranean, fennel is a much-appreciated vegetable. The raw bulbs have a refreshing crispness reminiscent of celery and a noticeable aniselike flavor. When cooked, they become tender and mild. To trim a fennel bulb, cut off the feathery fronds and stems and discard any tough or discolored outer layers from the bulb. Using a sharp knife, split the bulb lengthwise. Cut out the base of the core if it is thick and tough.

POTATOES LYONNAISE

In a large, nonstick frying pan over medium heat, melt 1 tablespoon of the butter with 1 tablespoon of the olive oil. Add the onion and sauté, stirring frequently, until golden brown and caramelized, 5–7 minutes. Transfer the onion to a bowl.

In the same frying pan over medium heat, melt ½ tablespoon each of the remaining butter and oil. Add half of the potato slices and cook, adding more butter or oil if needed, until the potatoes are browned on both sides, about 4 minutes. Transfer to the bowl with the onions. Repeat with the remaining butter, oil, and potatoes.

Return the onion and potatoes to the frying pan and add the stock. Raise the heat to high, cover, and boil for 2 minutes. Uncover the pan and boil until the liquid is reduced by three-fourths, about 3 minutes longer. Remove from the heat, stir in the parsley, and season to taste with salt and pepper. Spoon into a warmed serving bowl and serve at once.

Serving Tip: These potatoes are a good accompaniment to many meat dishes, including grilled beef, lamb, and veal chops.

MAKES 4 SERVINGS

POTATOES LYONNAISE

This well-known potato dish is named for Lyons, a city in central France renowned for its wealth of culinary resources, including high-quality produce (most notably onions), a dizzying array of sausages and cheeses, and one of France's favorite wines, Beaujolais. More specifically, the term *lyonnaise* refers to a dish made with sautéed onions and often a final sprinkling of chopped fresh parsley. To make this dish worthy of being served in any Lyons *bouchon*, or bistro, be sure to sauté the onions to a golden caramel brown.

2 tablespoons unsalted butter, plus extra as needed

2 tablespoons olive oil, plus extra as needed

1 large yellow onion, thinly sliced

10–12 small white or red potatoes, about 2 lb (1 kg) total weight, peeled and thinly sliced

½ cup (4 fl oz/125 ml) chicken stock (page 110) or prepared low-sodium broth

2 tablespoons finely chopped fresh flat-leaf (Italian) parsley

Salt and freshly ground pepper

POTATOES SAVOYARDE

3 tablespoons unsalted
butter, cut into small
pieces, plus 1 tablespoon,
melted

3 cloves garlic, minced

2 tablespoons finely
chopped fresh flat-leaf
(Italian) parsley

1½ cups (6 oz/185 g)
shredded Gruyère cheese

Freshly ground pepper

4–6 russet or Yukon gold
potatoes, about 2½ lb
(1.25 kg) total weight,
unpeeled and cut into
slices ¼ inch (6 mm) thick

1½ cups (12 fl oz/375 ml)
chicken stock (page 110)
or prepared low-sodium
broth

Preheat the oven to 375°F (190°C). Brush the bottom and sides of a 2-qt (2-l) baking dish with the melted butter. In a small bowl, stir together the garlic, parsley, cheese, and ¼ teaspoon pepper.

Layer one-third of the potatoes in the prepared dish, sprinkle one-third of the garlic-cheese mixture over the potatoes, and dot with 1 tablespoon of the butter. Repeat with half each of the remaining potatoes, garlic-cheese mixture, and butter. Top with the remaining potatoes. Pour the stock over the potatoes, sprinkle the rest of the garlic-cheese mixture evenly over the top, and dot with the remaining 1 tablespoon butter. Cover with buttered aluminum foil and bake for 30 minutes.

Remove the foil and continue baking, uncovered, until the top is browned and crusty and the potatoes are tender when pierced with a fork, 30–40 minutes longer. Serve at once.

MAKES 6 SERVINGS

POTATO GRATINS
Creamy potatoes dauphinoise is a well known dish, but this crusty version of potato gratin comes from the Dauphine's neighboring region of Savoy, where chicken or beef stock and a bit of butter moisten and enrich the potatoes. Gratins, a French specialty, are quickly recognizable by their crisp browned tops, often sprinkled with cheese or bread crumbs to give extra texture and flavor. Traditional gratin dishes are wide and just deep enough to allow a delicious contrast between the bubbling brown surface and the tender layers beneath.

SEAFOOD AND POULTRY

The corn-fed chickens of Bresse, the meaty ducks of Gascony, the briny scallops of Brittany, and the abundant seafood of Nice and Marseilles—all have inspired generations of French chefs to create new and delightful ways of preparing seafood and poultry. From a classic coq au vin to a hearty bouillabaisse, these are some of the best-loved dishes of French cuisine.

SOLE MEUNIÈRE
56

BOUILLABAISSE
59

ROAST SALMON WITH WARM LENTILS
60

COQUILLES SAINT-JACQUES PROVENÇALE
63

CHICKEN DIJONNAISE
64

COQ AU VIN
67

SAUTÉED DUCK BREASTS WITH LAVENDER HONEY
68

GRILLED QUAIL WITH HERB BUTTER
71

SOLE MEUNIÈRE

DREDGING
Dredging, or completely coating pieces—often thin fillets—of fish, meat, or poultry in seasoned flour or bread crumbs, slows the escape of moisture during sautéing or frying and helps create an appealing golden crust. One of the most common ways to dredge a fillet is to drag both sides through the dry ingredient in a shallow bowl. Shaking the foods in a large zippered plastic bag of flour is another quick, tidy way to dredge. Always dredge just before sautéing; if left to sit, the coating will soak up moisture and become gummy.

Put the flour in a shallow bowl or large zippered plastic bag and season with salt and pepper. Dredge the fillets in the seasoned flour *(left)*.

In a large frying pan over medium-high heat, melt 2 tablespoons of the butter with 1 tablespoon of the olive oil. Shake the excess flour from half of the fillets and add to the pan. Cook until golden on the bottom, about 2 minutes. Turn carefully and cook until golden on the second side, just tender when pierced with a fork, and opaque throughout, about 1 minute longer, depending on the thickness of the fillets. Transfer the fillets to a warmed platter and cover loosely with aluminum foil. Repeat with the remaining butter, olive oil, and fillets.

Add the lemon juice and parsley to the pan and stir over medium-high heat for 1 minute to allow the flavors to blend. Transfer the fillets to warmed individual plates and spoon some of the warm sauce over each serving. Serve at once.

MAKES 4–6 SERVINGS

½ cup (2½ oz/75 g) all-purpose (plain) flour

Salt and freshly ground pepper

8–10 sole fillets, about 2 lb (1 kg) total weight, skinned, rinsed, and patted dry

4 tablespoons (2 oz/60 g) unsalted butter

2 tablespoons olive oil

¼ cup (2 fl oz/60 ml) fresh lemon juice

2 tablespoons finely chopped fresh flat-leaf (Italian) parsley

BOUILLABAISSE

2 tablespoons olive oil

2 yellow onions, finely
chopped

2 carrots, peeled and finely
chopped

4 large cloves garlic, minced

1 large can (28 oz/875 g)
diced tomatoes, with juice

2 cups (16 fl oz/500 ml) dry
white or full-bodied red wine

2 cups (16 fl oz/500 ml) fish
stock (page 111)

2 wide pieces orange zest,
removed with a peeler

Pinch of saffron threads

1 lb (500 g) firm white fish
fillets such as halibut,
skinned, rinsed, and cut into
2-inch (5-cm) pieces

1 lb (500 g) mussels,
scrubbed and debearded
(page 22)

¾ lb (375 g) sea scallops,
cut in half horizontally

Salt and freshly ground
pepper

6–12 thin slices baguette,
lightly toasted

Rouille *(far right)* for serving

¼ cup (⅓ oz/10 g) finely
chopped fresh flat-leaf
(Italian) parsley

In a large soup pot over medium-high heat, heat the oil. Add the onions and sauté, stirring occasionally, until softened and very lightly browned, 5–7 minutes. Add the carrots and sauté until slightly softened, 4–5 minutes. Add the garlic and cook for 1 minute.

Add the tomatoes with their juice, wine, stock, and orange zest and bring to a simmer over medium heat. Cover partially and cook until the soup is highly aromatic and the vegetables are nicely softened, about 15 minutes.

Remove and discard the orange zest. In a blender or food processor, partially purée the soup in batches, making sure to leave some texture, and return the soup to the pot. Alternatively, process with a handheld blender in the pot.

Raise the heat to medium-high. Add the saffron, fish, and mussels, discarding any mussels that do not close to the touch. Cover and cook until the fish is opaque throughout and the mussels have opened, 6–8 minutes. Discard any mussels that have not opened. Add the scallops and cook until opaque throughout, about 2 minutes. Season to taste with salt and pepper.

Ladle the soup into warmed bowls, dividing the seafood evenly. Arrange 1 or 2 slices of toast on top of each serving and spoon a dollop of *rouille* onto each toast. Garnish with the parsley and serve at once.

MAKES 6 SERVINGS

ROUILLE

A garlicky mayonnaise with flecks of rusty red, *rouille* ("rust" in French) is a traditional accompaniment to bouillabaisse. To make *rouille*, combine 4 cloves garlic and 1 roasted, peeled, and finely chopped red bell pepper (capsicum) or pimiento in a blender or food processor and process until well blended. Add 1 cup (8 fl oz/ 250 ml) homemade or best-quality mayonnaise (page 111) and process until smooth. Season to taste with salt, black pepper, and cayenne pepper. Refrigerate the *rouille* in a covered container until ready to serve or up to 5 days. Makes 1¼ cups (10 fl oz/310 ml).

ROAST SALMON WITH WARM LENTILS

In a saucepan over medium-high heat, combine the lentils and 3¼ cups (26 fl oz/820 ml) of the stock and bring to a boil. Reduce the heat to medium-low, cover, and simmer until the lentils are tender but not mushy, about 30 minutes. (You may need to add a bit of water toward the end.) Drain and set aside.

In a frying pan over medium heat, heat 3 tablespoons of the olive oil. Add the onion and sauté until softened, 5–7 minutes. Add the celery and carrot and sauté until slightly softened, about 2 minutes. Add the bell pepper and sauté until softened, about 2 minutes.

Add the lentils to the pan and sauté over medium heat to allow the flavors to blend, about 2 minutes. Stir in the lemon juice, the remaining 1 tablespoon olive oil, the chopped parsley and basil, and salt and pepper to taste. Transfer 1 cup (7 oz/220 g) of the lentil mixture to a blender or food processor. Process to a purée, adding just enough of the remaining ¾ cup (6 fl oz/180 ml) stock to produce a saucelike consistency. Return to the pan with the whole lentils and mix well. Taste and adjust the seasoning. Cover, set aside, and keep warm.

Preheat the oven to 450°F (230°C). Season the salmon with salt and pepper. Place the fillets on a baking sheet and roast until just opaque throughout, about 12 minutes, depending on the thickness of the fillets.

Mound an equal amount of the lentils on each individual plate and place a salmon fillet on top of each mound. Garnish with the parsley sprigs and basil leaves and serve at once.

MAKES 6 SERVINGS

PUY LENTILS

The town of Le Puy, in the Auvergne region of eastern France, is famous for its tiny, olive green lentils, known as *lentilles du Puy,* or simply French lentils. The prized lentils are harvested in summer and traditionally dried under the hot local sun. Unlike the more common brown lentils, which can become very soft and lose their shape when cooked, French lentils keep their lens-like profile and subtle flavor, making them a favorite for lentil salads and side dishes.

¾ cup (5 oz/155 g) French green lentils, picked over, rinsed, and drained

4 cups (32 fl oz/1 l) chicken stock (page 110) or prepared low-sodium broth

4 tablespoons (2 fl oz/60 ml) olive oil

1 red onion, finely chopped

1 celery stalk, finely diced

1 carrot, peeled and finely diced

1 small red bell pepper (capsicum), seeded and finely diced

3 tablespoons fresh lemon juice

2 tablespoons finely chopped fresh flat-leaf (Italian) parsley, plus sprigs for garnish

2 tablespoons finely chopped fresh basil, plus small whole leaves for garnish

Salt and freshly ground pepper

6 salmon fillets, about ½ lb (250 g) each, skinned, rinsed, and patted dry

COQUILLES SAINT-JACQUES PROVENÇALE

5 tablespoons (2½ fl oz/
75 ml) olive oil

2 shallots, finely chopped

6 cloves garlic, minced

1 cup (6 oz/185 g) canned
crushed tomatoes, with
juice

½ cup (4 fl oz/125 ml) plus
2 tablespoons dry white
wine

1 tablespoon finely
chopped fresh flat-leaf
(Italian) parsley, plus sprigs
for garnish

1 tablespoon finely
chopped fresh basil

Salt and freshly ground
pepper

¼ cup (1½ oz/75 g)
all-purpose (plain) flour

1½ lb (750 g) sea scallops

In a large frying pan over medium-high heat, heat 2 tablespoons of the olive oil. Add the shallots and sauté until softened, about 2 minutes. Add the garlic and sauté until softened but not brown, about 1 minute. Add the tomatoes with their juice, the ½ cup wine, the chopped parsley, the basil, and salt and pepper to taste, and bring to a simmer. Reduce the heat to medium and cook until the sauce is slightly thickened, 3–5 minutes. Taste and adjust the seasoning. Set aside and keep warm.

Put the flour in a large zippered plastic bag and season with salt and pepper. Shake to mix well. Place the scallops in the bag and shake gently until the scallops are evenly coated with the flour.

In a large nonstick frying pan over medium-high heat, heat the remaining 3 tablespoons olive oil. Shake the excess flour from the scallops, place in the pan, and sauté, turning once, until golden brown on both sides and opaque throughout, about 2 minutes per side. Add the remaining 2 tablespoons wine and deglaze the pan, stirring to scrape up any browned bits. Add the tomato sauce and stir gently to coat the scallops. Transfer to a serving dish, garnish with parsley sprigs, and serve at once.

MAKES 4 SERVINGS

PROVENÇAL INGREDIENTS

Coquilles Saint-Jacques, the French name for sea scallops, is also the name of a classic method of preparation in which scallops are bathed in a creamy white wine sauce and gratinéed with cheese and bread crumbs. In this fresh Provençal version, the cream and cheese are replaced with tomatoes, olive oil, garlic, and basil. These Mediterranean flavors, popular throughout southern Europe, are closely identified with the cuisine of Provence, with its warm coastal climate and proximity to Italy.

CHICKEN DIJONNAISE

DIJON MUSTARD

To the French, the city of Dijon is held in high regard as the capital of Burgundy, one of the country's greatest wine-producing regions. However, to the rest of the world, Dijon is best known for its namesake condiment, Dijon mustard. Using a mixture of finely milled mustard-seed flour and *verjus,* the tart juice of unripe grapes, the mustard makers of Dijon produce more than half of the mustard of France, which is why dishes described as dijonnaise almost always contain mustard. If you like a grainy, coarse-textured mustard, look for jars labeled *à l'ancienne* or *en grains*.

In a large frying pan over medium-high heat, melt 2 tablespoons of the butter with 1 tablespoon of the olive oil. Add the chicken breasts and sauté, turning once, until golden brown on both sides, about 3 minutes per side. Transfer to a warmed platter and loosely cover with aluminum foil to keep warm.

Add the remaining 1 tablespoon each butter and olive oil to the pan over medium-high heat and heat until the butter is foamy. Add the shallots and sauté until softened, about 2 minutes. Add the wine, stock, and garlic and bring to a boil. Boil until the liquid is reduced to about ½ cup (4 fl oz/125 ml), about 2 minutes.

Whisk in the cream and mustard and return to a boil. Reduce the heat to medium and cook until the sauce is slightly thickened, about 3 minutes. Whisk in the tarragon, thyme, and salt and white pepper to taste. Taste and adjust the seasoning.

Return the chicken breasts and any collected juices to the pan and cook just until the chicken is heated and opaque throughout, about 5 minutes, depending on thickness. Do not overcook. Arrange the chicken breasts on warmed individual plates. Spoon over additional sauce, garnish with the parsley, and serve at once.

MAKES 4–6 SERVINGS

3 tablespoons unsalted butter

2 tablespoons olive oil

6 boneless, skinless chicken breast halves, about 6 oz (185 g) each

2 shallots, finely chopped

½ cup (4 fl oz/125 ml) dry white wine

1 cup (8 fl oz/250 ml) chicken stock (page 110) or prepared low-sodium broth

2 cloves garlic, minced

¾ cup (6 fl oz/180 ml) heavy (double) cream

3 tablespoons Dijon mustard, preferably whole grain

1 tablespoon finely chopped fresh tarragon or 1 teaspoon dried

1 teaspoon finely chopped fresh thyme or ½ teaspoon dried

Salt and freshly ground white pepper

2 tablespoons chopped fresh flat-leaf (Italian) parsley

COQ AU VIN

6 slices bacon, about 5 oz (155 g) total weight, cut into 1-inch (2.5-cm) pieces

¼ cup (1½ oz/45 g) all-purpose (plain) flour

Salt and freshly ground pepper

3 chicken breast halves, skin on and bone in

3 chicken thighs, skin on and bone in

3 chicken drumsticks

3 tablespoons olive oil

¼ cup (2 fl oz/60 ml) brandy

2 cups (16 fl oz/500 ml) full-bodied red wine

1 tablespoon tomato paste

3 cloves garlic, minced

½ lb (250 g) white button mushrooms, brushed clean and quartered

10 oz (315 g) frozen baby or pearl onions, thawed

2 tablespoons finely chopped fresh flat-leaf (Italian) parsley

In a large Dutch oven over medium heat, cook the bacon until crisp, 4–5 minutes. Using a slotted spoon, transfer to paper towels to drain. Pour off all but 1 tablespoon of bacon fat from the pot.

Put the flour in a large zippered plastic bag and season with salt and pepper. Shake to mix well. Place the chicken pieces in the bag (in batches if necessary) and shake until evenly coated.

Add 2 tablespoons of the olive oil to the pot with the reserved bacon fat and heat over medium-high heat. Shake the excess flour from the chicken. Add half of the chicken pieces to the pot and cook until evenly browned on all sides, 5–7 minutes. Transfer to a bowl and repeat with the remaining pieces.

Return the chicken to the pot off the heat. Pour the brandy over the chicken. Return to medium-low heat and cook to warm the brandy, about 30 seconds. Once again, remove the pan from the heat. Make sure the overhead fan is off and, averting your face, use a long kitchen match to ignite the brandy. When the alcohol has burned off, the flames will die out. (Keep a pan lid ready in case the flames flare up.) When the flames disappear, stir in the wine, tomato paste, and garlic and cover the pot. Bring to a simmer over medium-low heat and cook the chicken, turning the pieces once, until tender and opaque throughout, about 50 minutes.

Meanwhile, in a frying pan over medium heat, heat the remaining 1 tablespoon oil. Add the mushrooms and sauté until slightly softened, 3–5 minutes. Raise the heat to medium-high, add the onions, and cook, stirring occasionally, until lightly glazed and heated through, 2–3 minutes longer. Season with salt and pepper.

When the chicken is cooked and the sauce is slightly thickened, add the mushroom-onion mixture and the parsley and stir to combine. Taste and adjust the seasoning. Transfer to a serving platter and serve at once.

MAKES 4–6 SERVINGS

FLAMBÉING

Flambéing is most often thought of in its impressive tableside incarnation, with a sudden flare of blue flame leaping up from a liqueur-drenched pan of *bananes flambées* or cherries jubilee. However, flambéing is also an essential step in making coq au vin and other dishes and sauces using spirits. By rapidly burning off the volatile alcohol, flambéing infuses a dish with aroma and flavor, without the harshness of raw, high-proof spirits.

SAUTÉED DUCK BREASTS WITH LAVENDER HONEY

LAVENDER HONEY
Lavender honey is made from
the nectar of lavender flowers,
which grow in abundance in
Provence. Like wine, which
varies in flavor depending on
the grapes used, honey shifts
in flavor and color depending
on the nectar gathered by the
bees. Lavender flowers yield
honey with a delicate, floral-
herbal flavor evocative of the
golden hillsides of southern
France. Seek out imported
French lavender honey in
specialty-food stores, or look
for locally harvested lavender
honey at farmers' markets.

Place the duck breast halves between 2 pieces of waxed paper.
Using a heavy frying pan or the smooth side of a mallet, pound
the breasts to an even thickness. Using a very sharp knife, score
the duck skin in a crosshatch pattern, making sure not to cut into
the meat.

In a large nonstick frying pan over medium-high heat, melt 1 tablespoon of the butter. Add the duck breasts, skin side down, and
sauté until the skin is golden brown and very crisp, 5–7 minutes.
Turn over and sauté until medium-rare (somewhat soft but still
resistant when pressed in the center), about 5 minutes longer.
Transfer, skin side up, to a warmed platter. Set the frying pan aside.

Combine 1 tablespoon of the honey with the boiling water and stir
until the honey dissolves. Brush the skin side of the duck breasts
with the honey mixture and cover loosely with aluminum foil.

Pour off all but 2 tablespoons of the drippings from the pan and
heat over medium-high heat. Add the shallots and sauté until
softened, about 1 minute. Add the stock, the remaining 1 tablespoon honey, and the vinegar and raise the heat to high. Boil until
the mixture is reduced to a light glaze, about 3 minutes. Whisk in
the remaining 1 tablespoon butter to thicken and add sheen to
the sauce. Season to taste with salt and pepper.

Transfer the duck breasts to a cutting board. Slice thinly on the
diagonal against the grain and arrange on individual plates.
Spoon the sauce over the duck and serve at once.

*Notes: Purchase fresh duck breasts if possible, as the flavor is superior;
frozen breasts tend to become rubbery after thawing. Look for veal or
duck stock in the frozen-foods section of well-stocked markets.*

MAKES 2 SERVINGS

2 boneless duck breast
halves, about 1 lb (500 g)
total weight, skin on (see
Notes)

2 tablespoons unsalted
butter

2 tablespoons lavender
honey

1 tablespoon boiling water

2 shallots, minced

½ cup (4 fl oz/125 ml)
purchased veal or duck
stock (see Notes)

1 teaspoon red wine
vinegar

Salt and freshly ground
pepper

GRILLED QUAIL WITH HERB BUTTER

FOR THE HERB BUTTER:

4 tablespoons (2 oz/60 g) unsalted butter, at room temperature

1 clove garlic, minced

¼ teaspoon dried oregano

¼ teaspoon dried thyme

1 teaspoon finely chopped fresh flat-leaf (Italian) parsley

Salt and finely ground pepper

FOR THE MARINADE:

¼ cup (2 fl oz/60 ml) olive oil

2 tablespoons red wine vinegar

2 shallots, finely chopped

2 cloves garlic, minced

¼ teaspoon dried oregano

¼ teaspoon dried thyme

Salt and freshly ground pepper

8 quail, 4 oz (125 g) each, halved (see Note)

Fresh flat-leaf (Italian) parsley leaves for garnish

To make the herb butter, using a wooden spoon, combine the butter, garlic, oregano, thyme, parsley, and salt and pepper to taste until well incorporated. Transfer to a sheet of waxed paper, form into a log, wrap, and refrigerate for at least 30 minutes or for up to 3 days.

To make the marinade, in a small bowl, combine the olive oil, vinegar, shallots, garlic, oregano, thyme, and salt and pepper to taste. Put the quail in a large bowl or zippered plastic bag and add the marinade. Cover or seal and let marinate, turning occasionally, for 2–4 hours in the refrigerator.

Prepare a charcoal fire in an outdoor grill and let burn until the coals are covered with white ash. Leave the coals heaped in the center of the grill; do not spread them out. For a gas grill, preheat on high, then reduce the heat to medium. Alternatively, use a grill pan over medium-high heat. Lightly oil the grill rack or pan. Remove the quail from the marinade and arrange on the rack or pan. Grill, turning as needed for even browning, until the breast meat is just cooked through and shows no sign of pink and the juices run clear when a thigh is pierced with a knife, 10–12 minutes. Arrange on a platter and top each half-bird with a slice of herb butter. Garnish with the parsley leaves and serve at once.

Note: These tiny birds are very delicate in flavor and low in fat. Marinating brings out their unique flavor and helps ensure a juicy cooked bird. To halve a quail, cut along either side of the backbone with poultry shears to remove it, and use a large chef's knife to cut the bird in half lengthwise at the breastbone.

Serving Tip: Braised spinach makes a nice accompaniment for this dish.

MAKES 4 SERVINGS

COMPOUND BUTTER
Beurres composés, or "compound butters," are versatile mixtures of butter creamed with herbs and seasonings. Since they can be quickly prepared and keep well, they are usually made ahead of time, shaped into a log, wrapped in waxed paper, and refrigerated. Once firm, the butter can be sliced as needed to add richness and flavor to grilled meat dishes. In French restaurants, pats of *maître-d'hôtel* butter (with minced parsley, lemon juice, salt, and pepper) are often laid on grilled steaks just before serving. The butter can also be used as a base for tea sandwiches.

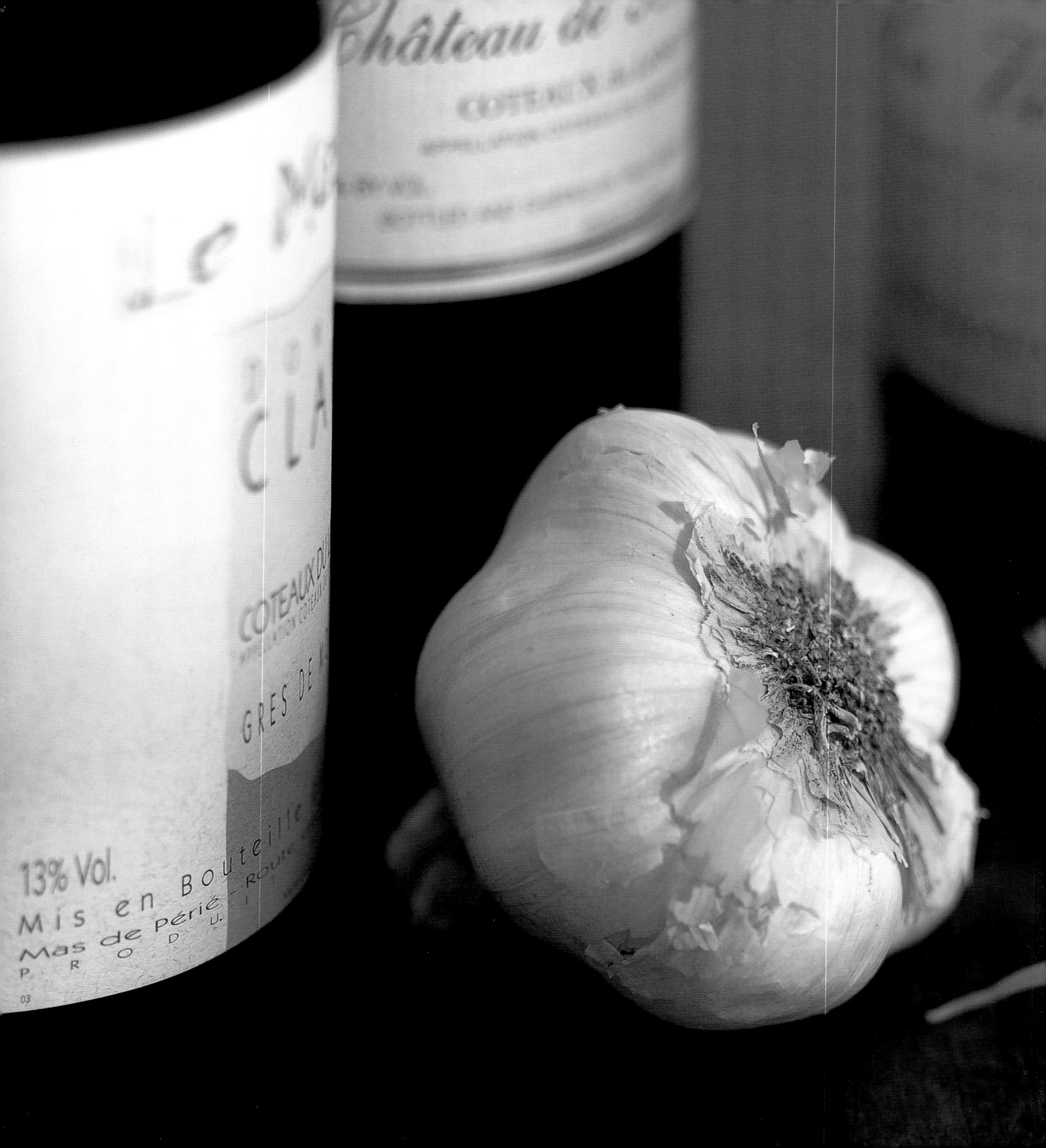
Château de
13% Vol.
Mis en
Mas de Périé

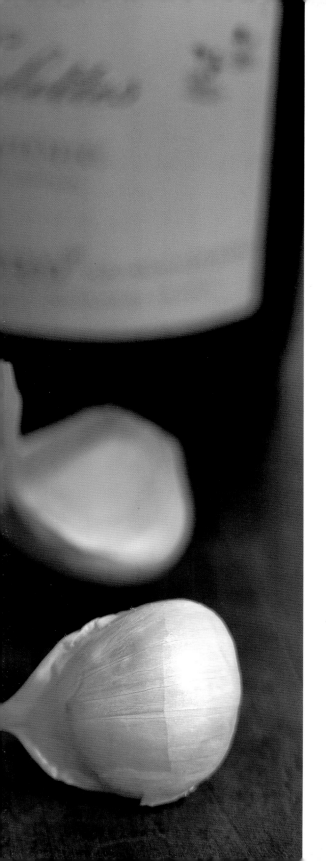

BEEF, VEAL, PORK, AND LAMB

Hearty and rich, the meat courses of France are as varied as its countryside. Inspired by the dairies and orchards of Normandy, pork loin is bathed in cream and Calvados, while France's most famous blue cheese tops filets mignons. Boeuf en daube melds the southern flavors of garlic, thyme, and tomato into a classic braise, and lamb shanks slow-cooked with prunes and served with couscous hint at North African influences.

GRILLED ENTRECÔTE
WITH MUSHROOM RAGOÛT

RAGOÛTS

The word *ragoût,* usually defined as a thick stew made with pieces of meat, poultry, fish, or vegetables—in this case, mushrooms—comes from the French verb *ragoûter,* which means to stimulate or revive the appetite. In most cases, the meat or vegetables are browned first and then added to the stew. This initial browning adds color and depth to the mixture, which also contains white or red wine and aromatic herbs such as parsley.

To make the ragoût, in a saucepan over medium-high heat, bring the wine and stock to a boil. Boil until the liquid is reduced to about 1¼ cups (10 fl oz/310 ml), 10–15 minutes. Set aside.

In a large frying pan over medium-high heat, melt the butter with the olive oil. Add the shallots and sauté until softened, about 3 minutes. Add the mushrooms and sauté until softened, about 5 minutes. Add the reduced wine mixture and bring to a simmer. Simmer until the mixture is syrupy, about 5 minutes. Add the cream, return to a simmer, and reduce the ragoût to a saucelike consistency, 2–3 minutes longer. Add the parsley and salt and pepper to taste. Set aside and keep warm.

Remove the steaks from the refrigerator 30 minutes before grilling. Prepare a charcoal fire in an outdoor grill and let burn until the coals are covered with white ash. Leave the coals heaped in the center of the grill; do not spread them out. For a gas grill, preheat on high, then reduce the heat to medium-high. Lightly oil the grill rack. Liberally season both sides of the steaks with salt and pepper. Arrange the steaks on the rack and sear for about 2 minutes. Using tongs, lift and rotate the steaks 90 degrees, then cook for 5–7 minutes longer. (This creates crosshatch marks.) Turn the steaks over and repeat on the second side, 7–9 minutes. The steaks should be almost charred on the outside and an instant-read thermometer should register 135°F (57°C) for medium-rare when inserted into the thickest part (but not touching bone).

Transfer the steaks to a platter, cover loosely with aluminum foil, and let rest for 10 minutes. Serve whole or cut against the grain into ½-inch (12-mm) slices. Top with the ragoût and serve.

MAKES 6 SERVINGS

FOR THE RAGOÛT:

1½ cups (12 fl oz/375 ml) full-bodied red wine

1 cup (8 fl oz/250 ml) beef stock (page 111), prepared low-sodium broth, or purchased veal stock

1 tablespoon unsalted butter

3 tablespoons olive oil

6 shallots, finely chopped

2 lb (1 kg) white button mushrooms, brushed clean and quartered

¼ cup (2 fl oz/60 ml) heavy (double) cream

2 tablespoons finely chopped fresh flat-leaf (Italian) parsley

Salt and freshly ground pepper

6 rib-eye steaks, each about 1½ lb (750 g) and 2 inches (5 cm) thick, with rib attached

Salt and freshly ground pepper

ROAST RACK OF LAMB PERSILLADE

2 racks of lamb, each 1½–1¾ lb (750–875 g) and with 7 or 8 chops, frenched (see Note) and trimmed of excess fat

1 cup (2 oz/60 g) coarse fresh bread crumbs *(far right)*

3 tablespoons olive oil

2 tablespoons chicken stock (page 110) or prepared low-sodium broth

2 shallots, finely chopped

¼ cup (⅓ oz/10 g) finely chopped fresh flat-leaf (Italian) parsley

Salt and freshly ground pepper

Fresh thyme sprigs or flat-leaf (Italian) parsley leaves for garnish

Preheat the oven to 450°F (230°C). If desired, wrap the ends of the bones with aluminum foil to keep from burning. Place the racks of lamb, bone side down, in a roasting pan, and roast until an instant-read thermometer inserted into the thickest part of the lamb (but not touching bone) registers 125°F (52°C) for rare or 135°F (57°C) for medium-rare, 18–25 minutes.

While the meat is roasting, in a small bowl, combine the bread crumbs, olive oil, stock, shallots, parsley, ¼ teaspoon salt, and ⅛ teaspoon pepper and mix well.

Preheat the broiler (grill). Pat the bread crumb mixture evenly on the meat side of the racks of lamb. Slide the lamb under the broiler and broil (grill) until the topping is lightly browned, 2–3 minutes. Watch carefully to prevent burning.

Transfer the racks to a cutting board. Slice into chops by cutting between the bones. Transfer the chops to a platter or arrange 2 or 3 chops on each individual plate. Garnish with the thyme and serve at once.

Note: Frenching is a technique in which meat is cut away from the top of a chop or rib to expose part of the bone. Ask your butcher to french the chops for you if not already done.

Serving Tip: For a pretty presentation, crisscross the bone ends of the lamb chops.

MAKES 4–6 SERVINGS

PERSILLADE

Persillade is a mixture of bread crumbs, parsley, and garlic or shallots moistened with butter or olive oil. Patted onto the lamb in this recipe and quickly browned under the broiler, the crumbs create a crisp, golden brown crust over the meat and the parsley adds a fresh, bright taste. To make fresh bread crumbs, lay slices of fresh French bread flat on a countertop and leave overnight to dry out. Or, use French bread a few days past its peak of freshness. Cut off the crusts, tear the bread into bite-sized pieces, and process in a blender or food processor to the desired texture.

VEAL MARENGO

Preheat the oven to 325°F (165°C). Rinse the veal and pat dry. Put the flour in a large, zippered plastic bag and season with salt and pepper. Shake to mix well. Place the veal in the bag and shake until evenly coated. Shake the excess flour from the veal.

In a large Dutch oven over medium-high heat, heat 2 tablespoons of the olive oil. Add half of the veal to the pot and cook until evenly browned on all sides, 4–5 minutes. Transfer to a bowl. Add 2 more tablespoons olive oil to the pot and repeat with the remaining veal.

Add 2 more tablespoons olive oil to the pot and heat over medium-high heat. Add the onion and sauté until lightly browned and softened, about 5 minutes. Add the garlic and sauté for 30 seconds. Add the wine and deglaze the pot, stirring to scrape up any browned bits. Add the tomatoes and their juice, basil, thyme, orange zest, and salt and pepper to taste and bring to a simmer. Return the veal to the pot and stir to combine.

Cover the pot, transfer to the oven, and roast until the meat is tender when pierced with a fork, about 1½ hours.

Toward the end of roasting, cook the mushrooms. In a frying pan over medium heat, heat the remaining 1 tablespoon olive oil. Add the mushrooms and sauté until softened, 4–5 minutes. Season to taste with salt and pepper.

Remove the pot from the oven, uncover, and discard the zest. Place over high heat. Bring to a boil and cook until the liquid is reduced by one-fourth and slightly thickened, 5–7 minutes. Add the mushrooms and 2 tablespoons of the parsley. Taste and adjust the seasoning. Serve the veal spooned over the noodles, garnished with the remaining 2 tablespoons parsley.

MAKES 4–6 SERVINGS

3 lb (1.5 kg) boneless veal stew meat, cut into 2-inch (5-cm) pieces

¼ cup (1½ oz/45 g) all-purpose (plain) flour

Salt and freshly ground pepper

7 tablespoons (3½ fl oz/ 105 ml) olive oil

1 yellow onion, finely chopped

2 cloves garlic, minced

1½ cups (12 fl oz/375 ml) dry white wine

1¼ cups (8 oz/250 g) canned crushed tomatoes, with juice

½ teaspoon dried basil

½ teaspoon dried thyme

1 wide piece orange zest, removed with a peeler

1 lb (500 g) white button mushrooms, brushed clean and quartered

4 tablespoons (⅓ oz/10 g) finely chopped fresh flat-leaf (Italian) parsley

¾ lb (375 g) egg noodles, cooked according to package instructions

FILETS MIGNONS WITH ROQUEFORT SAUCE

4 filet mignon steaks,
6–8 oz (185–250 g) each

Salt and freshly ground
pepper

3 tablespoons olive oil

2 cloves garlic, minced

¾ cup (6 fl oz/180 ml)
tawny Port

½ cup (4 fl oz/125 ml)
heavy (double) cream

¼ lb (125 g) Roquefort
cheese, crumbled

2 teaspoons finely
chopped fresh flat-leaf
(Italian) parsley

Liberally season both sides of the steaks with salt and pepper. Select a frying pan large enough to fit the steaks without crowding. Heat the olive oil over medium-high heat. Add the steaks and sear on one side until well browned, about 5 minutes. Turn the steaks and sear on the second side until well browned and an instant-read thermometer inserted into the thickest part registers 135°F (57°C) for medium-rare, about 3 minutes longer, depending on thickness. Transfer to a warmed platter and cover loosely with aluminum foil.

Add the garlic and Port to the pan and bring to a boil over high heat, stirring with a wooden spoon to scrape up any browned bits from the pan bottom. Boil until reduced to ⅓ cup (3 fl oz/80 ml), about 2 minutes. Whisk in the cream and return to a boil. Boil until reduced by half, about 2 minutes longer. Add the cheese and whisk until the cheese melts and the sauce is thickened, about 1 minute. Season to taste with salt and pepper.

Transfer the steaks to warmed individual plates and spoon the sauce over them. Garnish with the parsley and serve at once.

MAKES 4 SERVINGS

ROQUEFORT CHEESE
One of France's great blue cheeses, true Roquefort is made only from sheep's milk and is aged in limestone caves surrounding the village of Roquefort-sur-Soulzon in south-western France. The unique mold indigenous to the area gives this cheese its distinctive blue veining and ripe, mellow pungency. Look for a moist, yellow-to-ivory interior thickly spored with blue-green mold.

BRAISED LAMB SHANKS WITH RED WINE, DRIED FRUIT, AND HERBS

PRUNES

For centuries, prunes, or dried plums, have been a specialty of the Agen district of Bordeaux in France. Today, the majority of the prunes eaten in the United States are produced in California, but the most common plum for drying is still the *prune d'Agen,* introduced to California by the French in the mid-1800s. Throughout Bordeaux and Gascony, prunes are commonly used in savory as well as sweet dishes. Here, the combination of braised lamb with dried fruit also reflects growing North African influences in French cooking.

Preheat the oven to 325°F (165°C). Place the flour in a shallow bowl and dredge the lamb lightly in the flour. Season the shanks with salt and pepper. In a large Dutch oven over medium-high heat, heat 2 tablespoons of the olive oil. Add the lamb in 2 batches and cook until evenly browned on all sides, about 8 minutes. Transfer all the lamb to a large roasting pan.

Reduce the heat to medium and add the remaining 2 tablespoons olive oil to the Dutch oven. Add the carrots, onion, celery, basil, and thyme and sauté, stirring occasionally, until the vegetables are tender, 6–8 minutes. Add the garlic and cook for 1 minute.

Stir in the stock, wine, prunes, crushed tomatoes and juice, and tomato paste. Bring to a simmer over medium-high heat. Pour the sauce over the lamb in the roasting pan. Cover the pan tightly with aluminum foil and roast in the oven until the meat is very tender and beginning to fall off the bones, about 2 hours. (Adjust the roasting time for larger or smaller lamb shanks).

Transfer the lamb to a serving platter and cover loosely with aluminum foil. Skim the surface fat from the pan juices. Pour the juices into a saucepan and bring to a simmer over medium-high heat. Cook until the juices are reduced by half and a thick, sauce-like consistency has formed, about 20 minutes. Taste and adjust the seasoning. Pour the sauce over the lamb and serve at once.

Serving Tip: To make herbed couscous to accompany this recipe, prepare 1½ cups (9 oz/280 g) instant couscous according to the package instructions. Add 1 tablespoon finely chopped fresh mint and 2 tablespoons finely chopped fresh flat-leaf (Italian) parsley, and fluff with a fork to serve.

MAKES 6 SERVINGS

½ cup (2½ oz/75 g) all-purpose (plain) flour

6 lamb shanks, ¾–1 lb (375–500 g) each

Salt and freshly ground pepper

4 tablespoons (2 fl oz/60 ml) olive oil

2 carrots, peeled and finely chopped

1 yellow onion, finely chopped

1 celery stalk, finely chopped

3 tablespoons finely chopped fresh basil

2 tablespoons finely chopped fresh thyme

4 cloves garlic, minced

2 cups (16 fl oz/500 ml) chicken stock (page 110) or prepared low-sodium broth

2 cups (16 fl oz/500 ml) dry red wine

9 oz (280 g) moist pitted prunes, cut into bite-sized pieces

1 cup (6 oz/185 g) canned crushed tomatoes, with juice

3 tablespoons tomato paste

PORK LOIN WITH APPLES AND CALVADOS

2 pippin apples or other firm, tart apples, peeled, cored, and coarsely chopped

1 cup (8 fl oz/250 ml) Calvados or other apple brandy

4 tablespoons (2 oz/60 g) unsalted butter

2 tablespoons olive oil

1 boneless pork loin roast, about 3 lb (1.5 kg), tied (see Note)

Salt and freshly ground pepper

1 yellow onion, finely chopped

⅓ cup (3 fl oz/80 ml) heavy (double) cream

½ cup (4 fl oz/125 ml) beef or chicken stock (pages 110–11) or prepared low-sodium broth

2 tablespoons finely chopped fresh flat-leaf (Italian) parsley

In a bowl, combine the apples and Calvados. Let marinate for at least 30 minutes or for up to 1 hour.

In a large Dutch oven over medium-high heat, melt the butter with the olive oil. Liberally season the pork with salt and pepper. Add the pork to the pot and cook, turning with 2 large spoons or tongs, until evenly browned on all sides, about 5 minutes. Transfer to a platter and cover loosely with aluminum foil.

Add the onion to the pot and sauté until softened and browned, 4–5 minutes. Add half of the apple-Calvados mixture and stir to combine. Reduce the heat to low, add the pork, cover, and simmer over low heat until an instant-read thermometer inserted into the center of the pork registers 160°F (71°C), about 1 hour. Transfer the pork to a carving board, cover loosely with aluminum foil, and let rest for 10 minutes. Remove the string from the pork.

Meanwhile, add the remaining apple-Calvados mixture to the pot. Simmer for 2 minutes to cook off some of the alcohol. Add the cream and stock and simmer until the sauce has thickened, about 3 minutes longer. Taste and adjust the seasoning.

To serve, carve the pork against the grain into slices ½ inch (12 mm) thick and arrange the slices, slightly overlapping, on a warmed platter. Spoon the sauce over the pork. Garnish with the parsley and serve at once.

Note: A pork loin that is tied will cook more evenly and will yield a more uniform, attractive shape for carving. To tie a pork loin, fold any thin ends under the loin and secure with kitchen string, tying the string around the loin at 2-inch (5-cm) intervals.

MAKES 6–8 SERVINGS

CALVADOS

Normandy, which borders the English Channel in north-western France, is known for its wonderful apples and their spirited by-products: hard cider and Calvados. This potent apple brandy, distilled from cider, is the pride of Normandy and is used in many recipes, pairing especially well with pork. It is also drunk straight as an after-dinner *digestif*. During a heavy meal, a small shot of Calvados served between courses is referred to as *le trou normand,* or "the Norman hole," imbibed to revive the appetite between courses.

BOEUF EN DAUBE EN CASSEROLE

Put the flour in a large, zippered plastic bag and season with salt and pepper. Shake to mix well. Add the beef (in batches if necessary) and shake until evenly coated. Shake the excess flour from the beef. In a large Dutch oven over medium-high heat, heat 3 tablespoons of the olive oil. Add the beef to the pot in batches, and cook until evenly browned on all sides, 5–7 minutes per batch, adding more oil if needed. Transfer to a bowl. Preheat the oven to 350°F (180°C). Have ready six 2-cup (16 fl oz/500 ml) individual baking dishes or ramekins. Peel the medium carrots and thinly slice the carrots and onions.

Add 2 more tablespoons olive oil to the pot and heat over medium-high heat. Add the onion and sauté until softened, about 5 minutes. Add the vinegar and continue to sauté until the onions are nicely browned, about 3 minutes. Add the sliced carrots and sauté until they begin to soften, about 3 minutes. Add the garlic and sauté for 1 minute. Add the beef stock, wine, tomato paste, and thyme and bring to a boil over medium-high heat. Return the beef to the pot and stir to combine.

Cover the pot, put in the oven, and cook, stirring occasionally, until the meat is almost tender, about 1½ hours. Add the baby carrots and new potatoes, re-cover, and cook until the vegetables are tender-crisp and the beef is tender, about 30 minutes longer. Stir in the parsley. Taste and adjust the seasoning. Remove the stew from the oven and raise the oven temperature to 400°F (200°C).

Roll out the puff pastry sheets into two 12-by-14-inch (30-by-35 cm) rectangles. Cut out 6 rounds, each 1 inch (2.5 cm) larger than the tops of the dishes. Divide the stew among the dishes. Press a pastry round on top of and around each dish, making indentations along the rims. Brush the pastry with the egg mixture. Place the dishes on a baking sheet and bake until the pastry is puffed and golden brown, 20–24 minutes. Serve at once.

MAKES 6 SERVINGS

PUFF PASTRY

One of the glories of French baking, puff pastry is made by alternating paper-thin sheets of dough with equally thin layers of butter to produce a rich, flaky dough that is perhaps best known for its use in croissants.

When slipped into the oven, the dough literally puffs up to form several hundred ultrathin crisp pastry layers. Making the pastry from scratch involves careful folding, rolling, and waiting; happily, frozen puff pastry dough is a fine substitute. Look for a good-quality brand that includes real butter, and check any sell-by or use-by dates.

½ cup (2½ oz/75 g) all-purpose (plain) flour

Salt and freshly ground pepper

3 lb (1.5 kg) boneless beef chuck, cut into 1½-inch (4-cm) cubes

5 tablespoons (2½ fl oz/ 75 ml) olive oil, plus extra if needed

2 medium carrots

2 large yellow onions

¼ cup (2 fl oz/60 ml) red wine vinegar

4 cloves garlic, minced

1½ cups (12 fl oz/375 ml) beef stock (page 111) or prepared low-sodium broth

1 cup (8 fl oz/250 ml) full-bodied red wine

¼ cup (2 oz/60 g) tomato paste

Leaves from 2 sprigs fresh thyme or ¼ teaspoon dried

¾ lb (375 g) *each* baby carrots and new potatoes, cut into ½-inch (12-mm) chunks

2 tablespoons finely chopped fresh flat-leaf (Italian) parsley

1 package (17½ oz/545 g) frozen puff pastry, thawed

1 large egg beaten with 1 tablespoon water

DESSERTS

For sheer elegance, nothing tops the creations of a French pâtisserie. *But the desserts of French home cooks are much more modest, demonstrating the simple pleasures of crêpes, custards, and seasonal fruits, and, of course, the delight of chocolate mousse. A cheese course offers a sophisticated alternative, with its intriguing combinations of fruits, nuts, savories, and wine.*

THE CHEESE COURSE

PAIRING CHEESE AND WINE

One of the best reasons for serving a cheese course is to prolong the enjoyment of the wine during a meal. Traditionally, the cheese course begins with the most mild cheese, paired with the wine drunk at dinner. As the cheeses progress in strength, you can begin pouring a sweeter fortified wine, such as Port, a traditional accompaniment to big, pungent cheeses such as Roquefort. Remember that lighter, fresher cheeses go best with white wines; more robust cheeses, especially hard cheeses, go better with reds.

While French desserts are world-famous, the final course of a traditional French meal is often a platter of carefully selected local cheeses. Here are some tips and selected combinations *(right)* to help you assemble an authentic French cheese course.

Focus on no more than 3 or 4 cheeses. One approach is to choose a firm aged cheese, a soft, young mild cheese and/or a goat's milk cheese, and a blue cheese. Try to aim for balance between aged, assertive cheeses and mild or creamy cheeses. Buy cheese freshly cut rather than prepackaged, and bring to room temperature before serving (cold cheese will be stiff and lack full flavor). Serve cheeses on a tray, board, or platter that can easily be passed from person to person, and provide small spreaders for soft cheeses and a cheese plane or sharp knife for harder cheeses.

It is perfectly fine to serve a cheese course with nothing more than a sliced baguette, but adding a few inventive accompaniments will elevate your selection from a simple cheese plate to a full-fledged course.

Fruit is the most typical accompaniment, and fresh grapes, ripe pears, and crisp apples will enhance nearly any cheese. Dried fruits, from apricots to prunes to figs, offer a sweet counterpart as well, especially in cold weather. Walnuts, almonds, and hazelnuts (filberts), served in the shell with a nutcracker and pick, or shelled and lightly toasted, are also customary accompaniments.

Finally, chunky, lightly sweetened conserves, such as apricot, peach, or sour cherry, make interesting matches with cheeses, especially if served with a savory, rustic bread. A drizzle of honey and soft, sweet-spicy quince paste are also excellent additions.

SERVE ABOUT 3 OZ (90 G) TOTAL CHEESE PER PERSON

SPRING SELECTION:

Saint-Nectaire (a medium-firm cow's milk cheese), Montrachet (a mild goat's milk cheese), and Bleu de Bresse (a mild blue cow's milk cheese)

Lavender honey, fresh strawberries, and apricot bread or baguette for serving

SUMMER SELECTION:

Fourme d'Ambert (a semi-soft, mild blue cow's milk cheese), Banon (a mild cow's or goat's milk cheese), and Saint-André (a soft cow's milk cheese)

Fresh Kadota or black Mission figs, oven-roasted tomatoes, and rosemary bread for serving

AUTUMN AND WINTER SELECTION (SHOWN OPPOSITE):

Young Crottin de Chavignol (a mild goat's milk cheese), Reblochon (a semisoft cow's milk cheese), and Roquefort (a blue sheep's milk cheese)

Chestnut honey, ripe pears or black grapes, quince paste *(membrillo),* toasted walnuts, and country-style or rye bread for serving

CRÈME BRÛLÉE

3 cups (24 fl oz/750 ml) heavy (double) cream

1 tablespoon pure vanilla extract (essence)

6 large egg yolks

⅔ cup (6 oz/185 g) sugar

Preheat the oven to 300°F (150°C). Place six ¾-cup (6-fl oz/180-ml) ramekins in a shallow roasting pan.

In a saucepan over medium-high heat, combine the cream and vanilla. Cook until small bubbles appear around the edges of the pan, about 5 minutes. Remove from the heat, cover, and let stand for about 15 minutes to infuse the cream with the vanilla.

In a bowl, whisk the egg yolks with ⅓ cup (3 oz/90 g) of the sugar until pale yellow, 2–3 minutes. Slowly whisk the warm cream mixture into the egg yolk mixture.

Pour the egg yolk–cream mixture through a fine-mesh sieve into the ramekins, dividing it evenly. Pour simmering water into the roasting pan to come one-third of the way up the sides of the ramekins. Cover the pan with aluminum foil.

Bake until the custards are set but the centers jiggle slightly when the ramekins are gently shaken, about 40 minutes. Remove from the oven and let cool in the water bath, then lift out the ramekins. Cover and refrigerate for at least 4 hours or for up to overnight.

Just before serving, remove the custards from the refrigerator and transfer to a baking sheet. Using a fine-mesh sieve, sift the remaining ⅓ cup sugar over the tops of the custards to form a thin, even layer. Using a kitchen torch, and holding it about 2–3 inches (5–7.5 cm) from the surface, caramelize the sugar by constantly moving the flame over the top until the sugar bubbles, about 30 seconds. Alternatively, preheat the broiler (grill). Slide the baking sheet under the broiler 3 inches (7.5 cm) from the heat source and broil (grill), turning the ramekins to cook the sugar evenly, until the tops are caramelized, about 1 minute. Serve immediately.

MAKES 6 SERVINGS

CUSTARD SAVVY

From *pot de crème* to flan to crème brûlée, all baked custards follow a few simple rules. Heat the cream gently until it is steaming hot but not boiling, to keep a skin from forming. To prevent the eggs from curdling, gradually whisk in the warm cream. Pouring the finished custard mixture through a sieve before baking will remove any lumps and smooth out any air bubbles. Finally, baking the custard in a water bath provides moist, even heat that prevents the mixture from turning tough or rubbery.

COLD LEMON SOUFFLÉ

Fit a 4-cup (32–fl oz/1-l) soufflé dish with a collar *(left)*. In a stainless-steel or glass bowl, using an electric mixer on medium speed, beat the egg yolks, sugar, and lemon zest until thick, about 2 minutes. In a small saucepan, bring the lemon juice to a simmer. Slowly add to the yolk mixture while stirring constantly. Beat the mixture on medium speed until it falls in a thick ribbon when the beaters are lifted, about 10 minutes.

In another small saucepan, sprinkle the gelatin over the water and let soften for about 5 minutes. Heat over low heat until the gelatin dissolves; do not allow to boil. Stir into the egg yolk mixture.

Using a balloon whisk or an electric mixer on medium-high speed, lightly whip 1 cup (8 fl oz/250 ml) of the cream in a chilled bowl until soft peaks form. Set aside. In a separate, large, spotlessly clean bowl, using a clean balloon whisk or mixer on medium-high speed, beat the egg whites until stiff peaks form. Set aside.

Nest the bowl holding the egg yolk mixture in a larger bowl partially filled with ice cubes and water and stir gently until it begins to thicken, 6–8 minutes. Carefully fold in the whipped cream and egg whites. Pour into the prepared soufflé dish. The mixture should come to the top of the collar. Refrigerate until firm, about 2 hours.

When ready to serve, beat the remaining ½ cup (4 fl oz/125 ml) cream until stiff peaks form. Carefully remove the collar from the soufflé and spread half of the whipped cream on top. Spoon the remaining cream into a pastry (piping) bag fitted with a small star tip and pipe rosettes of cream around the edge. Gently press the pistachios into the sides of the soufflé and serve.

Note: This dish includes uncooked eggs. See page 113.

MAKES 4–6 SERVINGS

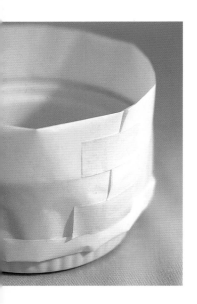

MAKING A COLLAR
To make a collar, cut a strip of parchment (baking) or waxed paper about 2 inches (5 cm) longer than the circumference of the soufflé dish. Fold the strip in half lengthwise and seal the open edge by folding it over, forming a 1-inch (2.5-cm) flap. Tape or tie the paper around the soufflé dish so that it rises 2 inches (5 cm) above the rim. Using a collar allows you to fill the dish above the rim, allowing this frozen dessert to mimic the puff of a traditional oven-risen soufflé.

4 large eggs, separated

1 cup (8 oz/250 g) sugar

3 tablespoons finely grated lemon zest

½ cup (4 fl oz/125 ml) fresh lemon juice

1½ tablespoons unflavored gelatin

¼ cup (2 fl oz/60 ml) water

1½ cups (12 fl oz/375 ml) heavy (double) cream

½ cup (2½ oz/75 g) finely chopped pistachios or almonds

CHERRY CLAFOUTIS

1 cup (8 oz/250 g) granulated sugar

3 cups (1 lb/500 g) pitted fresh sweet cherries or thawed frozen cherries

1 cup (5 oz/155 g) all-purpose (plain) flour

1 teaspoon baking powder

Pinch of salt

4 large eggs

1¾ cups (14 fl oz/430 ml) half-and-half (half cream)

2 teaspoons pure vanilla extract (essence)

Grated zest of 1 lemon

Confectioners' (icing) sugar for dusting

Preheat the oven to 425°F (220°C). Butter a 9-by-13-inch (23-by-33-cm) baking dish. Place the baking dish on a baking sheet. Sprinkle the bottom of the dish with 2 tablespoons of the granulated sugar. Spread the cherries in the bottom of the dish and bake for 10 minutes. There may be a lot of juice; do not drain. Set aside.

In a bowl, whisk together the flour, baking powder, and salt. In a large bowl, using an electric mixer on medium speed, beat the eggs with ¾ cup (6 oz/185 g) of the granulated sugar until blended, about 1 minute. Add the flour mixture in 2 additions, alternating with the half-and-half in 1 addition. Add the vanilla and lemon zest and stir to combine.

Pour the batter over the cherries. Sprinkle with the remaining 2 tablespoons granulated sugar. Bake until puffed and golden brown, 30–35 minutes. Transfer to a wire rack to cool slightly. Using a fine-mesh sieve, dust the top with confectioners' sugar and serve.

MAKES 6–8 SERVINGS

CHERRY CLAFOUTIS
This homey dessert has a comforting, spongy texture somewhere between a baked custard and a thick crêpe. As prepared in Limousin, the region in central France where it originated, the thick batter is studded with plump, unpitted black cherries. This recipe, however, suggests using pitted sweet cherries such as Bings. Remove the pits with a small, sharp knife or use a cherry pitter. If fresh cherries are unavailable, you can use frozen cherries.

CRÊPES SUCRÉES WITH GRAND MARNIER

GRAND MARNIER

This elegant, Cognac-based liqueur, whose original recipe dates back to 1880, lends a complex orange perfume to a wide variety of French desserts. True Grand Marnier is made from aromatic bitter orange peels macerated and distilled with French Cognac and aged for 8 months. A little goes a long way, and its incomparable flavor shines in this simple but striking dessert. Other orange-flavored liqueurs that could be substituted here include Triple Sec and Cointreau.

To make the batter, in a blender, combine the water, milk, eggs, flour, sugar, and vanilla. Blend until very smooth. Refrigerate, covered, for at least 1 hour or up to 1 day.

Lightly grease a nonstick 9-inch (23-cm) crêpe or frying pan and place over medium heat. Pour 2–3 tablespoons batter into the pan and swirl the pan to cover the bottom with batter. Cook until the crêpe begins to bubble and brown a little and is set, about 1 minute. Flip the crêpe carefully with a spatula and cook for another 10 seconds, until slightly browned and set. Transfer to a piece of waxed paper. Repeat to make 8 crêpes total, stacking the finished crêpes between pieces of waxed paper.

Fold each of the crêpes in half, then in half again, to form a triangle.

In a large, nonstick frying pan over medium heat, melt 2 tablespoons of the butter with 2 tablespoons of the sugar and half of the orange zest. Heat until the butter is melted and foamy, 1–2 minutes. Remove from the heat and add half of the Grand Marnier to the pan. Stir to combine and return to the heat for about 1 minute. Place 4 crêpe triangles in the pan and heat for about 1 minute on each side, turning them with tongs to coat evenly. Place 2 crêpes on each of 2 warmed dessert plates and divide the sauce between the servings. Repeat with the remaining 4 crêpes and ingredients. Accompany each serving with a scoop of vanilla ice cream.

MAKES 4 SERVINGS

FOR THE CRÊPES:

½ cup (4 fl oz/125 ml) water

½ cup (4 fl oz/125 ml) whole milk

2 large eggs

1 cup (5 oz/155 g) all-purpose (plain) flour

2 teaspoons sugar

1 teaspoon pure vanilla extract (essence)

4 tablespoons (2 oz/60 g) unsalted butter, plus extra for greasing

4 tablespoons (2 oz/60 g) sugar

Grated zest of 1 orange

½ cup (4 fl oz/125 ml) Grand Marnier

French vanilla ice cream for serving

TARTE TATIN

FOR THE PASTRY:

1 cup (5 oz/155 g)
all-purpose (plain) flour

1 tablespoon sugar

Pinch of salt

½ cup (4 oz/125 g) very
cold unsalted butter, cut
into 1-inch (2.5-cm) pieces

¼ cup (2 fl oz/60 ml) ice
water

FOR THE APPLES:

6 tablespoons (3 oz/90 g)
unsalted butter

¾ cup (6 oz/185 g) sugar

5 or 6 pippin or Granny
Smith apples, 2–2½ lb
(1–1.25 kg) total weight,
peeled, cored, and
quartered

French vanilla ice cream or
crème fraîche (page 113)
for serving

To make the pastry, in a food processor, combine the flour, sugar, and salt. Pulse for a few seconds to blend. Add the butter and process until the mixture resembles coarse meal, 5–10 seconds. With the motor running, slowly add the ice water and process just until the dough comes together and adheres when pinched. Transfer the dough to a floured work surface and bring together in a rough mass. Press into a disk and roll out into an 11-inch (28-cm) round. Place between 2 pieces of waxed paper and refrigerate until well chilled, at least 2 hours.

To make the apples, preheat the oven to 400°F (200°C). In a nonstick 10-inch (25-cm) ovenproof frying pan over medium heat, melt the butter. Add the sugar and stir until combined, about 2 minutes. It may look a little lumpy. Arrange the apple quarters, round sides down, in the bottom of the pan, using just enough apples so that they fit very snugly in a single layer. Reduce the heat to low and cook until the caramel is brown and the apples are slightly tender, about 15 minutes.

Transfer the frying pan to the oven and bake the apples for 5 minutes. Remove with oven mitts, place on a trivet, and let cool for 10 minutes. Raise the oven temperature to 450°F (230°C). Carefully place the pastry round over the apples, using a small knife to tuck the excess pastry inside the rim of the pan. Bake until the pastry is crisp and golden brown, about 20 minutes.

Carefully remove the frying pan from the oven. Run a knife around the edge of the pan to loosen the tart. Place a 12-inch (30-cm) serving platter upside down on top of the pan. Wearing oven mitts, quickly invert the pan and platter together. Be careful, as the pan and juices will be very hot. Lift off the pan. Serve warm or at room temperature with vanilla ice cream.

MAKES 6–8 SERVINGS

PASTRY BASICS

For a tender, flaky pastry, start with well-chilled ingredients and handle the dough as little as possible to avoid developing the gluten in the flour (the culprit in tough or leathery pastry). Every batch of pastry will take a slightly different amount of water, depending on the dryness of the flour and the humidity of the day. Add just enough water to make the dough come together. Letting the dough rest in the refrigerator before using helps prevent shrinkage while making the dough easier to roll out. For the simplest cleanup, roll the dough out between 2 sheets of waxed paper.

CHOCOLATE MOUSSE

CHOCOLATE VARIETIES
Different chocolate varieties are defined by how much chocolate liquor they contain, which also determines the depth of their chocolate flavor. Bittersweet and semisweet usually contain nearly the same amount of chocolate liquor along with cocoa butter and sugar. Bittersweet is more commonly used in Europe, and semisweet is typically slightly sweeter. Either can be used in this recipe. Not all chocolate varieties are interchangeable. For this recipe, do not use unsweetened or baking chocolate, which is 100 percent liquor, or milk chocolate, which contains milk solids.

In a heatproof bowl or the top pan of a double boiler, combine the chocolate and butter. Set over (but not touching) barely simmering water and melt slowly. Stir to combine. Remove the bowl or top pan and set aside. Let cool.

In a small bowl, combine the ¼ cup crème fraîche and the egg yolks and beat until well blended. Add to the cooled chocolate mixture.

In a large, spotlessly clean bowl, using a balloon whisk or an electric mixer on medium-high speed, beat the egg whites with the salt until stiff peaks form. Using a rubber spatula, gently fold about one-fourth of the egg whites into the chocolate mixture to lighten it, then gently but thoroughly fold in the remaining whites, making sure there are no lumps. Pour into a 4-cup (32–fl oz/1-l) serving bowl and refrigerate until completely set, 2–4 hours.

When ready to serve, accompany each serving with a spoonful of crème fraîche, if using, and garnish with the chocolate curls.

Notes: This dish includes uncooked eggs. For more information, see page 113. To make decorative chocolate curls, use a vegetable peeler to shave a bar of chocolate. Use different parts of the bar to vary the width of the curls. To ensure long curls, the chocolate must be at room temperature. You can also use a cheese grater or Microplane to grate chocolate for a simpler garnish.

MAKES 6 SERVINGS

8 oz (250 g) bittersweet or semisweet (plain) chocolate, coarsely chopped

1 cup (8 oz/250 g) unsalted butter, cut into pieces

¼ cup (2 oz/60 g) crème fraîche, plus ⅓ cup (3 oz/90 g) for optional garnish (page 113)

3 large egg yolks

6 large egg whites

Pinch of salt

Chocolate curls for garnish (see Notes)

FRENCH BASICS

French chefs have long been admired around the world, and cooks from San Francisco to Singapore, seduced by both presentation and flavor, regularly try to reproduce their dishes at home. But French food is more than the sophisticated menus of famous chefs. It is a cuisine of contrasts, a mixture of unparalleled refinement and everyday cooking, of foie gras and French fries.

BRIEF HISTORY

France is arguably home to the world's most distinguished cuisine. The French table, made up of a vast web of regional specialties, owes this celebrated reputation to four basic factors: respect for tradition, superior ingredients, skilled chefs, and discriminating diners. Indeed, the average French citizen grows up learning about food and expecting it to be of high quality, whether it is the everyday dishes of a farmhouse kitchen, the popular plates of a provincial bistro, or the exalted cuisine of a four-star Paris restaurant.

Yet good French cooking, regardless of the setting, also depends on the mastery of fundamental cooking techniques, from sauce making to sautéing. Simply put, the same rule applies if you are preparing haute cuisine or the home-style recipes in this book: learning the basics is the first step.

EQUIPMENT

Gleaming saucepans; a ceramic jar bristling with assorted spoons, whisks, and ladles; white porcelain baking dishes; shiny fluted tart pans, and brightly glazed ceramic ramekins—these are the elements that stock the French kitchen of many cooks' dreams. While it is true that a well-chosen *batterie de cuisine* is the foundation of any good kitchen, you can make all the recipes in this book using just a small roster of commonplace equipment. Here, you'll find a list of everything you are likely to need.

Every French kitchen is stocked with at least one very good frying pan or sauté pan. These two pans are generally interchangeable, but traditionally a frying pan differs from a sauté pan in that it has sides that flare outward, making it useful for cooking foods that must be stirred or turned out of the pan.

Also known as a straight-sided frying pan, a sauté pan is deeper than a frying pan but wider than a saucepan. Designed to help you toss foods being cooked without their tumbling out over the rim, a sauté pan is also useful for braised dishes and other stove-top recipes that call for a large proportion of stock or sauce.

If you want to master the art of sautéing (page 107), a sauté pan is a good investment. Ideally, select one that has a high-mounted handle and relatively high sides. However, a frying pan can usually be used in any recipe calling for a sauté pan. Whichever pan you choose, make sure it is made from quality materials. Stainless steel and anodized aluminum are two good choices.

A good-quality saucepan is also essential to any French kitchen. This simple, round pan with straight or sloping sides can be used for everything from making sauces and soups to blanching vegetables and boiling potatoes. The pan's shape encourages rapid evaporation so that a sauce or liquid reduces quickly and efficiently. A 2-quart (2-l) size is the most useful for home cooks. Saucepans come in a variety of materials including stainless steel, anodized aluminum, copper, and enameled cast iron.

A Dutch oven, a thick and heavy lidded pot that holds and distributes heat slowly and evenly, is indispensable for making long-cooked stews and braises such as Coq au Vin (page 67) and Boeuf en Daube en Casserole (page 86). An enameled cast-iron Dutch oven is a particularly good investment, as the enamel lining won't react with acidic ingredients and doesn't demand the careful care and seasoning required by regular cast iron. Dutch ovens can go from stove top to oven. They come in a range of sizes, but a 7- to 9-quart (7- to 9-l) pot is the most versatile.

In addition to the pans listed above, you may also want to acquire some special French bakeware, including a soufflé dish. Straight-sided, round, and usually made of white porcelain with a distinctive "pleated" exterior and a narrow rim, a soufflé dish gives just the right support for its light, airy contents. Although these dishes come in a variety of sizes, the recipes in this book call for only two: a 4-cup (32–fl oz/1-qt/1-l) and a 6-cup (48–fl oz/1.5 qt/1.5-l) size.

Many French recipes call for ramekins for making individual-sized portions. These small, round ceramic baking dishes are similar to soufflé dishes, but are only 3 to 4 inches (7.5 to 10 cm) in diameter.

Any kitchen stocked for French cooking should have at least two whisks: one for sauces and one for whipping egg whites and heavy cream. Long, narrow, and shaped a bit like a baseball bat, a basic sauce whisk is a crucial tool in making vinaigrettes, custards, and cream sauces, as its rigid wires move rapidly through the mixture and help it to emulsify and thicken evenly. The whisk will beat out lumps faster and more thoroughly than a spoon, as well. A second type of sauce whisk, with a flat head of wire loops, is also handy for sauces.

While it may be faster and some-times easier to beat egg whites or heavy cream with an electric mixer, you will ultimately have more control, and a loftier final product, if you do it by hand. For egg whites and cream, use a balloon whisk, whose thinner wires expand into a rounded ball. This distinctive shape helps incorporate the maximum amount of air into the ingredients being whipped.

For information on the double boiler, tart pan, and mandoline, see the glossary on pages 113–15.

INGREDIENTS

French cooks have an enormous respect for ingredients. Even the French way of grocery shopping illustrates this reverence for acquiring the best materials for cooking. Unlike some countries, where large super-markets offer one-stop shopping, in France the preference is to purchase different ingredients from separate specialized shops and street markets. The freshest bread may be found at a *boulangerie,* while choice cuts of meat at a *boucherie.* Similarly, fresh produce, cheeses, and wines are all purchased from individual vendors to ensure the highest-quality ingredients.

When cooking the recipes in this book, follow this example and use the best ingredients you can find. Seeking out a fruity extra-virgin olive oil to add to a vinaigrette, or using the freshest cream and finest vanilla in a crème brûlée, will make a marked difference. Also, always keep in mind when choosing a recipe that produce is most flavorful at the height of its season. Asparagus will never taste better than in early springtime, and cherries are at their sweetest in summer.

TECHNIQUES

From deglazing a pan to whisking a vinaigrette, most French cooking techniques are not difficult to master. Once you've practiced tossing ingredients in a sauté pan, or watched closely while a sauce reduces and thickens, these methods will begin to become second nature.

SAUTÉING

A term derived from the French verb *sauter*, "to jump," sautéing is a classic cooking method of the French kitchen. Although it is often used as a synonym for frying, true sautéing does indeed make the food "jump" in the pan. Pushing and pulling the pan back and forth in a brisk motion, with a slight lift on the "away" push, will make the food within bounce lightly and roll over toward the center of the pan. Keeping the food moving in this way ensures fast, even cooking.

Finely chopped onions and shallots are almost always sautéed as a first step, which mellows their harsh bite and brings out their sweetness. Tender, boneless cuts of chicken and fish fillets as well as scallops and other seafood also benefit from a quick sauté, either to brown them quickly or to cook them through evenly before they can toughen.

To practice the back-and-forth sauté motion, start with a pan and a handful of dried beans. Without using heat, try making the beans "jump" over onto themselves as you pull and push the pan toward and away from you. Once you've mastered the motion, try it over heat with a simple food item, such as potato cubes.

When sautéing, be sure to dry the food well, and to cut it into small pieces or thin slices, so that it cooks quickly. To prevent sticking, preheat the pan briefly over medium to medium-high heat, then add the oil (and butter, if using). When you can smell the fragrance of the fat cooking and tiny bubbles appear around the edges of the pan, add the food to be sautéed. It's also a good idea to sauté in batches if there is a possibility the pan will be too crowded. An overfilled pan will trap moisture, steaming the food and resulting in a final product that is soft and soggy, instead of browned and crisp.

MAKING SAUCES

Perhaps more than any other cuisine, French cooking is defined by its grand array of sauces. But each sauce is not unique from start to finish; instead, almost all French sauces are developed out of a handful of so-called mother sauces. Once you understand how the components of these basic sauces come together, you will be able to master a wide variety of different sauces, and then maybe even invent some of your own.

A vinaigrette is perhaps the simplest of French sauces, and there is no mystery to making a good one. First, make sure to use a bowl big enough to allow you to whisk vigorously. Start with good-quality vinegar or citrus juice, then add seasonings such as minced herbs. Slowly drizzle in the oil—extra-virgin olive oil and buttery hazelnut and walnut oils are all good choices—whisking constantly until the mixture emulsifies, becoming semiopaque and thickened. Adding a small amount of finely minced shallot or a teaspoon of mustard to the vinegar will help the dressing to thicken. Finally, season with salt and pepper. It's best to whisk your vinaigrette again just before using; most dressings separate upon standing.

Creamy, elegant white sauces are one of the hallmarks of French cooking. They often begin with a roux, a mixture of butter and flour. The roux is cooked over medium heat for 2 to 3 minutes, just long enough to eliminate its raw taste. The mixture must not be allowed to brown. When milk is added to a roux, it becomes béchamel sauce, which is the basis for most savory soufflés, including the Cheese Soufflé on page 21. The sauce is simmered on low heat for a few minutes until thickened and smooth. If the sauce doesn't thicken right away, let it cook for a few more minutes, stirring constantly with a whisk. Velouté sauce is made the same way as béchamel, but a light chicken or fish stock is substituted for the milk.

Pan sauces are another common French sauce preparation. The richly caramelized bits clinging to the pan after a steak is pan-seared or a chicken breast is sautéed are quickly loosened with wine or stock in a step known as deglazing. Then, over medium-high or high heat, the alcohol evaporates and the liquid reduces and thickens. Mustard, herbs, or other flavorings may be added, and, at the last minute, a bit of butter or cheese may be swirled in, adding a silky finish to the completed sauce. The basic steps are shown opposite:

1 **Browning the food:** Sear or sauté the meat, chicken, or fish—here a filet mignon—until nicely browned on both sides, then remove from the pan.

2 **Deglazing the pan:** Add liquid—here Port—and bring to a boil over high heat, stirring with a wooden spoon to dislodge any browned bits stuck to the pan bottom.

3 **Reducing the sauce:** Continue to boil until the sauce is reduced as directed—here to ⅓ cup (3 fl oz/80 ml)—then whisk in any additions, such as crème fraîche or cream (shown here).

4 **Finishing the sauce:** If the recipe calls for reducing further, continue to boil as directed, in this case until reduced by half. Whisk in any final ingredients—such as crumbled cheese—and cook until smooth and thickened.

Sweet sauces represent the final category of French sauces addressed in this book. They include egg-based custard sauces, such as the one used to make Crème Brûlée (page 93). This mixture of eggs and cream is cooked just until the proteins in the ingredients thicken to form a soft, smooth, satiny dish. To prevent the eggs in the custard sauce from curdling, never add hot liquid all at once to beaten eggs. Instead, "temper" the eggs by slowly whisking in the warm cream or milk. By adding the liquid gradually, you will raise the temperature of the eggs and the rest of the liquid can be safely added. Baked custards should always be cooked in a water bath (also known as a *bain marie*) to keep them moist. For the silkiest custard, strain the mixture through a sieve before baking.

COOKING WITH WINE

With its distinctive character and affinity for robust flavors, wine plays a starring role in many classic French dishes, including Coq au Vin (page 67) and Boeuf en Daube en Casserole (page 86). You don't need to splurge on a rare vintage to make these dishes; instead, look for respectable, well-priced French or domestic wines.

Cooking with wine follows a simple rule that should never be broken: use only wines that you would be happy to drink. Look for wines that are well balanced between fruit and tannins (the compounds derived from grape skins that add a dry, puckery taste reminiscent of well-steeped tea). In red wines, search for flavors such as red grapes, plums, or berries, and in white wines, green apples, green grapes, apricots, or peaches. Grape varietals such as Merlot, Cabernet Sauvignon, or Pinot Noir, all of which produce dry, well-flavored wines, are excellent both for cooking and drinking. Zinfandel, an American varietal, is a big, bold red that works well with beef and lamb. Sauvignon Blanc and Pinot Gris grapes produce light, pleasantly crisp white wines that go particularly well with seafood. Chardonnay grapes, grown in Burgundy, produce some of the great white wines of France, including those from Chablis, Mâcon, Meursault, and Montrachet. French Chardonnay tends to be leaner and racier than the sweet, buttery Chardonnay bottled in California. For cooking, a drier white wine usually works best.

PAIRING WINE AND FOOD

No book on French cooking would be complete without a section on pairing wine and food. "Red with meat, white with fish" is a useful tip to start any consideration of matching wine and food, but it should not be taken as a hard-and-fast rule. It's easy to see the natural pairings—a deep, richly flavored red wine such as a Cabernet Sauvignon with a sturdy winter dish such as Boeuf en Daube en Casserole (page 86) or Grilled Entrecôte with Mushroom Ragoût (page 74), or a golden Chardonnay with delicate Sole Meunière (page 56). But many dishes can pair equally well with a red or a white wine, depending on the weather, the mood of the diners, and the rest of the menu. Roast Salmon with Warm Lentils (page 60) or the robustly flavored Coquilles Saint-Jacques Provençale (page 63), for example, would marry as well with a dry rosé as with a rounded, vigorous white wine.

A bubbling flute of golden Champagne is a typical French way to begin a meal, especially as an aperitif with an hors d'oeuvre such as Caramelized Onion Tart (page 26) or Rillettes de Canard (page 29). It can also match the celebratory nature of a perfectly puffed Cheese Soufflé (page 21).

A fruity, mellow Merlot would pair well with Sautéed Duck Breasts with Lavender Honey (page 68) or Braised Lamb Shanks with Red Wine, Dried Fruit, and Herbs (page 82). Pork Loin

with Apples and Calvados (page 85) could be matched with either a light red, such as a young Pinot Noir, or a perfumed white wine, such as a Riesling or a French Chardonnay.

Serve white wines chilled, but not too cold, as a little warmth is needed to release their flavors and aromas. An ideal temperature is between 40° and 50°F (4° and 10°C). Champagne and other sparkling wines should always be served cold. Chill white and sparkling wines in the refrigerator for up to 2 hours, or for about 20 minutes in an ice bucket.

Red wine, by contrast, should not be served too warm, which can make it taste flat. The best temperature is "cellar temperature," 55° to 65°F (13° to 18°C). Before serving a young red wine that is particularly high in tannins, opening it up and letting it "breathe" for 10 to 15 minutes can sometimes improve its quality. Very old wines often develop a murky sediment at the bottom of the bottle and may need to be decanted before serving.

Wine should be stored in a cool, dark place away from heat and light. Wine that you plan to age should always be stored on its side. This keeps the cork wet; a dry cork lets in oxygen, which will spoil the wine.

BASIC RECIPES

Here are some of the basic recipes referred to throughout this book.

CHICKEN STOCK

1 bouquet garni (page 113)

6 lb (3 kg) chicken necks and backs

3 celery stalks

3 carrots, peeled

2 yellow onions, halved and root ends cut off

2 leeks, white and pale green parts only, rinsed (page 45) and sliced

In a large stockpot, combine the bouquet garni, chicken parts, celery, carrots, onions, leeks, and cold water just to cover (about 3½ qt/3.5 l). Slowly bring to a boil over medium heat. Reduce the heat to as low as possible and simmer, uncovered, for 3 hours, using a spoon or skimmer to skim off the foam from the surface regularly.

Strain the stock through a colander into a bowl. Let cool for about 1 hour, then cover and refrigerate for at least 30 minutes. Using a large spoon, remove the hardened fat from the surface and discard it.

Cover and refrigerate the stock for up to 3 days, or pour into airtight containers or zippered plastic freezer bags and freeze for up to 3 months. Makes about 3 qt (3 l).

FISH STOCK

2 tablespoons vegetable oil

2 lb (1 kg) heads, skin, bones, and flesh of fresh white-fleshed fish, such as halibut or sea bass

1 yellow onion, thinly sliced

2 carrots, unpeeled and cut into 2-inch (5-cm) pieces

6 fresh flat-leaf (Italian) parsley stems

2 celery stalks with leaves, cut into 2-inch (5-cm) pieces

1 bay leaf

10 white peppercorns

5 fresh dill sprigs

1 lemon, thinly sliced

In a large stockpot over low heat, warm the oil and sauté the fish parts for 2–3 minutes. Do not let them brown. Add all the remaining ingredients with cold water just to cover (about 3½ qt/3.5 l). Bring to a boil over medium-high heat. Reduce the heat to low and simmer, uncovered, for 45 minutes, using a spoon or skimmer to skim off the foam from the surface regularly.

Line a fine-mesh sieve with cheesecloth (muslin) and pour the stock through it into a bowl. Let cool for about 1 hour, then cover and refrigerate for at least 30 minutes. Using a large spoon, remove the hardened fat from the surface and discard it.

Cover and refrigerate the stock for up to 3 days, or pour into airtight containers or zippered plastic freezer bags and freeze for up to 3 months. If frozen, reboil before using. Makes about 3 qt (3 l).

BEEF STOCK

4 lb (2 kg) beef bones with some meat attached

2 large carrots, cut into 2-inch (5-cm) slices

1 large yellow onion, cut into 2-inch (5-cm) slices

2 leeks, white and pale green parts only, rinsed (page 45) and cut into 2-inch (5-cm) chunks

1 bouquet garni (page 113)

Preheat the oven to 425°F (220°C). Place the beef bones in a large roasting pan and roast until browned, about 1½ hours, stirring a few times to color the bones evenly.

Remove the pan from the oven. Transfer the bones to a large stockpot. Add about 3 cups (24 fl oz/750 ml) water to the roasting pan and place it over medium-high heat. Bring to a boil and deglaze the pan, stirring to scrape the browned bits from the bottom of the pan. The water will become a rich brown.

Transfer the contents of the roasting pan to the stockpot and add cold water (about 3½ qt/3.5 l) just to cover the bones. Add the carrots, onion, leeks, and the bouquet garni.

Slowly bring to a boil over medium heat, reduce the heat to as low as possible, and simmer, uncovered, for 4 hours, using a spoon or skimmer to skim off the foam from the surface regularly.

Turn off the heat and let the stock cool for 30 minutes. Remove and discard the bones. Line a fine-mesh sieve with cheesecloth (muslin) and pour the stock through it into a bowl. Let cool to room temperature, then cover and refrigerate for 2 hours.

Using a large spoon, remove the hardened fat from the surface and discard it.

Line the sieve with clean cheesecloth, and pour the stock through it again to make sure it is fat free. The stock should be clear. Cover and refrigerate the stock for up to 3 days, or pour it into airtight containers or zippered plastic freezer bags and freeze for up to 3 months. Makes about 3 qt (3 l).

BASIC MAYONNAISE

2 large egg yolks

Salt and freshly ground white pepper

1 cup (8 fl oz/250 ml) canola oil or grapeseed oil

1½ teaspoons fresh lemon juice

In a bowl, using a whisk or a handheld electric mixer, beat the egg yolks until thick, 1–2 minutes. Beat in 1 teaspoon salt and a pinch of white pepper. While whisking constantly, slowly add the oil, drop by drop, scraping down the sides of the bowl as needed, until an emulsion forms.

When half of the oil has been added, begin adding the remaining oil in a slow, very thin stream. Continue whisking until all the oil is used and the mayonnaise is thick. Beat in the lemon juice. Cover and refrigerate for 2 hours to blend the flavors. The mayonnaise will keep for up to 5 days. Makes about 1 cup (8 fl oz/250 ml).

Note: This recipe contains raw egg. For more information, see page 113.

GLOSSARY

BOUQUET GARNI This bundle of aromatic herbs is frequently used to flavor stocks and sauces. The typical French bouquet garni combines parsley, thyme, and bay leaves. The herbs are tied together before using so that they can be easily removed from the finished dish. To make a bouquet garni for use in the stock recipes in this book, place 4 fresh flat-leaf (Italian) parsley sprigs, 2 fresh thyme sprigs, and 1 bay leaf on a square of cheesecloth (muslin), bring up the corners, and tie securely with kitchen string.

BREAD CRUMBS, FRESH See page 77.

CAPERS Caper bushes grow wild throughout southern France and around the Mediterranean. Before they can flower, the small, olive green buds are harvested and preserved in salt or a vinegar brine. Pleasantly tangy, capers add a piquant bite to Provençal dishes. Salt-packed capers have a slightly more pungent bite and are worth seeking out. They should be rinsed and drained before using.

CHERVIL This lacy herb, with its delicate parsley-anise flavor, is best known as a component of *fines herbes,* a fresh blend of chervil, parsley, tarragon, and chives, most commonly used in sauces and in omelets. Chervil wilts quickly; to keep, wrap in a damp paper towel, place in a plastic bag, and store in the refrigerator for 1–2 days.

COGNAC This double-distilled brandy is made only in the Charente and Charente Maritime areas in western France. Smooth and potent, Cognac derives its distinctive flavors from the region's chalky soil, where the grapes are grown, and from the Limousin or Tronçais oak barrels used for aging. Cognac is labeled according to barreling age: V.S. (Very Special) has been aged for at least 2 years, while V.O. (Very Old), V.S.O.P. (Very Special Old Pale), and Réserve have been finished in wood for at least 4 years. Cognacs labeled X.O., Vieille Réserve, or Hors d'Age have been aged for at least 6 years, although many top-quality Cognacs are aged up to 20 years or more. The words *Grande Fine Champagne* on the label denote that 100 percent of the grapes used were grown in the vineyards designated Grande Champagne, in the area near the town of Cognac. *Fine Champagne* indicates that more than 50 percent of the grapes were grown in the Grande Champagne region.

CRÈME FRAÎCHE A soured cultured cream product originally from France, crème fraîche is similar to sour cream but sweeter and milder with a hint of nuttiness. It may be purchased, or you may make your own. Combine 1 cup (8 fl oz/250 ml) heavy (double) cream and 1 tablespoon buttermilk in a saucepan over medium-low heat. Heat to lukewarm; do not allow to simmer. Remove from the heat, cover, and allow to thicken at warm room temperature until it is as thick and flavorful as you like, from 8 to 48 hours. Refrigerate to chill it before using.

CRÊPE PAN This extremely shallow pan, with its flat base and severely sloping sides, is just big enough—usually 9 inches (23 cm)—to cook one crêpe at a time. The long, flat handle ensures ample leverage for flipping the crêpes, while the flat base and low sides make it easy to spread the batter in an even circle by rotating the pan.

DOUBLE BOILER Used for gentle cooking, warming, or melting, a double boiler is made of two pots, one fitting on top of the other, outfitted with one lid that fits both pots. A small amount of water is brought to a simmer in the bottom half, while ingredients are placed in the top half to heat gently. The food is warmed by the heat of the steam. A double boiler is used when direct heat could scorch or curdle delicate ingredients, such as when melting chocolate or making egg-based sauces.

EGG, RAW Eggs are sometimes used raw or partially cooked in sauces and other preparations. These eggs run a risk of being infected with salmonella or other bacteria, which can lead to food poisoning. This risk is of most concern to small children, older people, pregnant women, and anyone with a compromised immune system. If you have health and safety concerns, do not consume undercooked eggs.

EGGS, SEPARATING Eggs are easier to separate when cold. Carefully crack each egg and, holding it over a bowl, pass the yolk back and forth between the shell halves, letting the whites fall into the bowl. Drop the yolk into a separate bowl, and transfer the whites to a third bowl. Separate each additional egg over an empty bowl, for if any speck of yolk gets into the whites, they will not whip up properly. If a yolk breaks, start fresh with another egg.

FRISÉE Pale, spiky leaves of frisée are a common ingredient in French salads, especially the famous Salade Frisée aux Lardons (page 37), in which the greens are mixed with chunks of cooked unsmoked bacon, dressed in a mustardy vinaigrette, and topped with a poached egg. Faintly bitter, this salad green is an immature version of curly endive, also known as chicory. It comes from the same family as escarole, Belgian endive (chicory/witloof), and radicchio.

GELATIN An odorless, colorless, taste-less thickener derived from collagen, gelatin is a protein extracted from the bones, cartilage, and tendons of animals. Two forms of gelatin are available: powdered gelatin, popular with American cooks, and sheet or leaf gelatin, which is commonly used in Europe. Both need to be hydrated and melted before they can be added to a recipe. Do not confuse unflavored powdered gelatin with the sweetened, fruit-flavored gelatin desserts sold in boxes.

JULIENNE See page 38.

LEEKS, RINSING See page 45.

MANDOLINE This narrow, rectangular tool, usually made of stainless steel, is used for slicing and julienning. It sits at an angle on the work surface, and the food to be cut is slid over a mounted blade. Some mandolines come with an assortment of blades that will produce a variety of shapes and thicknesses. This handy tool simplifies the task of creating thin, uniform slices, especially for dishes such as Potatoes Lyonnaise (page 50) and Pommes Frites (page 17).

NONALUMINUM It is best not to use aluminum cookware for preparing dishes that contain acidic ingredients, such as tomatoes, citrus juice, vinegar, wine, and leafy green vegetables. The acids in these foods can react with the metal and give the finished dish an off flavor or darkened color. Instead, use cookware made of or lined with a nonreactive material, such as stainless steel, enamel, or glass, or use anodized aluminum cookware.

NUTMEG The pit of a tropical fruit, this aromatic spice has a peppery, pungent flavor popular in both sweet and savory dishes. Often dusted on top of baked custard, grated nutmeg also adds a pleasant edge to cream sauces and cooked spinach. Preground nutmeg loses its taste and aroma quickly; instead, buy whole nutmegs and grate them as needed. Inexpensive metal nutmeg graters, often with a compartment to hold a whole nutmeg or two, are sold at kitchenware stores.

OLIVE OIL A staple of Mediterranean cooking, olive oil is both delicious and healthful. France, Spain, Italy, Greece, California, and Australia all produce high-quality olive oils. Extra-virgin oils are pressed without the use of heat or chemical solvents. Depending on the location and type of olive, the color of these oils can range from a rich gold to a murky deep green. Show off the rich flavor of extra-virgin olive oil by using it uncooked in vinaigrettes, as a seasoning, or as a condiment. "Pure" olive oil is extracted from a subsequent pressing, usually by means of heat or chemicals, and generally has a less distinctive olive flavor. It is often labeled simply "olive oil" and is good for general cooking, frying, or sautéing. Olive oil will solidify at cold temperatures; store it in a cool dark place rather than in the refrigerator.

PARSLEY, FLAT-LEAF Flat-leaf parsley, also called Italian parsley, has a more complex and refreshing flavor than curly leaf parsley. Although curly leaf parsley makes a decorative garnish, it imparts little distinctive flavor to a dish. For best results, always use fresh flat-leaf parsley for cooking.

PEPPER, WHITE White and black peppercorns start off as the same berries on the tropical pepper bush. Berries used for black peppercorns, however, are harvested when slightly underripe and dried with their hulls on, while berries for white peppercorns are fully ripened and their dark hulls are removed before drying. The result is a pale tan peppercorn with a slightly milder flavor than its black counterpart. Because of their pale color, ground white peppercorns are used for seasoning cream sauces and other light-colored dishes.

PORT A full-bodied fortified wine, Port is a classic after-dinner drink or a wonderful accompaniment to a cheese course. Named for the place from which it was first shipped, the city of Porto, in northern Portugal, Port is available in three types: sweet ruby Port, as red as its name; amber-colored, drier tawny Port; and aged vintage Port, rich and complex, which can age well for decades.

SHALLOTS These small members of the onion family have delicate lavender-veined lobes under papery gold skins. Milder than onions, shallots turn sweet and mellow when cooked, and they are used in many recipes where the harsher flavor of onion would be overpowering.

TARRAGON With its slender, deep green leaves and elegant, slightly anise-like scent, tarragon is among the most beloved herbs in the French garden. Along with chives, parsley, and chervil, it is an essential ingredient in a *fines herbes* mixture and is frequently used with fish and chicken. It is also a good addition to a homemade or prepared mayonnaise.

TART PAN Tarts are baked in pans with shallow, usually fluted vertical sides. They come in a variety of sizes. Look for one with a removable bottom, which allows you to free a tart easily from its pan. To remove the finished tart, place the pan on a large can or canister and let the sides fall away.

THYME Sprinkle a chicken with a spoonful of *herbes de Provence* or drop a bouquet garni into a simmering stew and you'll release the evocative fragrance of this Mediterranean herb. Wild thyme—tiny, oval, dark green leaves on low scrubby bushes—is an integral part of the *maquis*, the aromatic blanket of tough plants that cover the windswept hillsides along the Mediterranean coast.

VANILLA EXTRACT The long, skinny brown bean of a tropical orchid, true vanilla has a deliciously sweet scent and a luscious, rounded flavor that melds perfectly with sweet custards, mousses, and soufflés. Pure vanilla extract (essence) is made from vanilla beans steeped in water and alcohol. For the most intense perfume, look for pure

extracts made from beans from Tahiti or Madagascar. Imitation vanilla has a thin, chemical flavor that dissipates quickly, and it should be avoided. Always let hot foods cool off for a few minutes before adding vanilla extract; otherwise, the heat will evaporate the alcohol, and along with it some of the vanilla flavor.

VINEGAR *Vinaigre*, the French word for vinegar, means "sour wine." After an initial fermentation turns the grape juice into wine, a second bacterial fermentation turns the wine's alcohol into acid, creating wine vinegar. Red wine and white wine vinegars are the most commonly used vinegars in French cooking, although Italian balsamic vinegar is gaining in popularity. True balsamic vinegar is made only from the pure wine must (or unfermented juice) of white Trebbiano grapes. The best balsamic is aged for several years in a series of casks made of different woods. Deep brown, syrupy, and very expensive, long-aged balsamic is used as a condiment in tiny amounts. For salad dressings and other everyday uses, look for a younger balsamic vinegar, aged less than 10 years. Be sure to read the bottle's label before you buy: many inexpensive balsamic vinegars are simply wine vinegars sweetened and darkened with sugar and caramel coloring. Because of its high acidity, vinegar has a long shelf life and does not need to be refrigerated. Do not substitute distilled white vinegar, made from grain alcohol, for the white wine vinegars, as it is tart but tasteless.

INDEX

SIMON & SCHUSTER SOURCE
A Division of Simon & Schuster, Inc.
Rockefeller Center
1230 Avenue of the Americas
New York, NY 10020

WILLIAMS-SONOMA
Founder and Vice-Chairman: Chuck Williams

WELDON OWEN INC.
Chief Executive Officer: John Owen
President: Terry Newell
Chief Operating Officer: Larry Partington
Vice President, International Sales: Stuart Laurence
Creative Director: Gaye Allen
Series Editor: Sarah Putman Clegg
Editor: Heather Belt
Designer: Teri Gardiner
Production Director: Chris Hemesath
Color Manager: Teri Bell
Production Assistant: Libby Temple

Weldon Owen wishes to thank the following people
for their generous assistance and support in producing
this book: Contributing Writer Stephanie Rosenbaum;
Copy Editor Carrie Bradley; Consulting Editor Sharon Silva;
Food Stylists Kim Konecny and Erin Quon; Assistant Food
Stylist Kris Hoogerhyde; Recipe Consultant Peggy Fallon;
Photographer's Assistant Faiza Ali; Proofreaders
Desne Ahlers and Arin Hailey; Production Designer
Joan Olson; and Indexer Ken DellaPenta.

Set in Trajan, Utopia, and Vectora.

Williams-Sonoma Collection *French* was
conceived and produced by Weldon Owen Inc.,
814 Montgomery Street, San Francisco,
California 94133, in collaboration with
Williams-Sonoma, 3250 Van Ness Avenue,
San Francisco, California 94109.

A Weldon Owen Production
Copyright © 2003 by Weldon Owen Inc. and
Williams-Sonoma Inc.

For information regarding special discounts for
bulk purchases, please contact Simon & Schuster
Special Sales at 1-800-456-6798 or
business@simonandschuster.com

Color separations by Bright Arts Graphics
Singapore (Pte.) Ltd.
Printed and bound in Singapore by Tien Wah
Press (Pte.) Ltd.

First printed in 2003.

10 9 8 7 6 5 4 3

Library of Congress Cataloging-in-Publication
data is available.

ISBN 0-7432-4994-1

A NOTE ON WEIGHTS AND MEASURES

All recipes include customary U.S. and metric measurements. Metric conversions are based on
a standard developed for these books and have been rounded off. Actual weights may vary.